WELFARE PROGRAMS:
AN ECONOMIC APPRAISAL

Third in the second series of Rational Debate Seminars
sponsored by the American Enterprise Institute
held at
The George Washington University
Washington, D. C.

WELFARE PROGRAMS: AN ECONOMIC APPRAISAL

James Tobin
W. Allen Wallis

RATIONAL DEBATE SEMINARS

American Enterprise Institute
for Public Policy Research
Washington, D. C.

Library of Congress Catalog Number 68-29092

FOREWORD

The American Enterprise Institute is pleased to present this learned discussion of another major public issue, "Welfare Programs: An Economic Appraisal." In this third Rational Debate in the 1967-68 series, Yale University Professor James Tobin and Rochester University President W. Allen Wallis examine the pros and cons of expanding or contracting the United States' increasingly significant activities in the field of welfare.

Other Rational Debates in the 1967-68 academic year featured Senator Paul H. Douglas and British Conservative Member of Parliament J. Enoch Powell discussing "How Big Should Government Be?"; University of Chicago Professor R. H. Coase and Columbia University Dean of Journalism Edward W. Barrett debating "Educational TV: Who Should Pay?"; and Justice Paul C. Reardon of the Supreme Judicial Court of Massachusetts with *New York Times* Managing Editor Clifton Daniel on "Fair Trial and Free Press."

September 18, 1968   William J. Baroody
                                  President
                                  American Enterprise Institute
                                    for Public Policy Research

PREFACE

One of the major issues facing the new President of the United States in 1969 will be the future of government welfare programs.

We are fortunate to have two able students of the problem, Yale University Professor James Tobin and Rochester University President W. Allen Wallis to examine components of the problem in this Rational Debate. We are hopeful that the views of these two men, and their discussions with the panel of experts, will make an important contribution to the continuing dialogue on welfare.

September 17, 1968

G. Warren Nutter
Coordinator
Rational Debate Series

CONTENTS

FIRST LECTURE

JAMES TOBIN

In 1967 Americans received from their governments, federal, state, and local, $49 billion of income for which they provided during the year no productive services in return. These governmental "transfer payments" amounted to 8 percent of total personal income. The growth of governmental transfer payments in the postwar period is indicated by the fact that they amounted to $14 billion, or 6.3 percent, of personal income in 1950. Nor are direct income transfers the full measure of public outlays designed to raise the real incomes of families and individuals. Governments also give aid by providing certain goods and services free or below market prices: important examples of such assistance are food stamps, medicare and other programs for public payment of costs of medical care, and subsidies of rent and mortgage interest. Whether in one way or the other, government effects a transfer of income and consumption from taxpayers to those individuals and families who meet the criteria eligibility for benefits in cash or kind.

These transfers I take to be the subject of our discussion, our rational debate. What is the rationale of making income transfers? How do some individuals obtain rights to benefits for which other citizens are not eligible? What *should* be the standards of eligibility? Should benefits be in cash or in kind? What is the proper division of responsibility for transfer programs among federal, state, and local governments?

I shall discuss, in particular, the relation of governmental income transfers to the problem of poverty. One purpose of the massive income transfers that now occur is to meet the basic needs of Americans who would otherwise be unable to obtain enough food or shelter or medical care to live at standards the society regards as tolerable minima. Yet, large as they are, governmental transfer programs have failed to eliminate poverty or its symptoms from the wealthiest and most affluent society in the history of the world. Nearly one-fifth of the American people fall below the standards of consumption officially accepted as defining poverty, about $3,200 a year for an urban family of four. Most of the official poor—perhaps three-quarters of them—receive no governmental assistance at all.

These facts are a source of bewilderment and frustration to taxpayers who feel heavily burdened by large and growing "welfare" expenditures. But the paradox is only superficial. Most transfer benefits go to people who are not poor, even to people who would not be poor in the absence of the benefits. Need is neither a necessary nor a sufficient criterion of eligibility for existing benefits programs. This is intentional, not accidental. As a nation, we have consciously refused to confer rights to benefits on the basis of need alone, and we have deliberately conferred these rights on entirely other criteria.

The principle that government has, on behalf of the society, an obligation—if only as a last resort—to relieve hunger and illness has a long tradition in this country. During the Great Depression, when it became evident that the task was beyond the capacities of local governments and private philanthropy, state and federal governments reluctantly assumed the obligation. But the commitment to it has always been diluted, and it still is today, by several other ethics of political economy that command widespread allegiance in the American people.

The most important of these is that reward should be scaled to effort, that he should not eat who does not work. Although many Americans regard this ethic as an ultimate principle of social justice, it also contains a large instrumental or utilitarian component—that is, the hard unpleasant work of the world will not get done if people who don't do it nevertheless can enjoy its fruits. In obedience to this principle, income transfer programs in the U. S. generally do not confer rights to benefits on the basis of need except when the society is satisfied that there are legitimate, excusable reasons for the need. Relief of those who are unreasonably needy is left to private charities and local relief officers.

Our national system of social insurance and welfare

payments was designed in the thirties, and it is no accident that the emphasis is on social security. The Great Depression showed how fragile and insecure the prosperity of an individual can be in a complex interdependent society. Not even the most prudent and the most self-reliant can protect himself against the hazards of life. Anyone can lose his job, grow old, become ill or disabled, be widowed or orphaned.

The New Deal's social security system was designed to protect people against severe loss of income in these contingencies, and with the passage of time the system has been extended to cover more people more adequately against more contingencies. Insecurity is not the same thing as need. Social insurance can keep poor people from being made poorer by disaster, and it can also protect relatively affluent Americans from interruptions to their style of life. It cannot help the chronically poor, those who have acquired nothing to feel insecure about in the first place.

The system is a strange and pragmatic amalgam of insurance and outright assistance. Rights to social insurance benefits can be earned only by prior contributions, but there is no rigid connection between the value of the contributions made by or for an individual and the actuarial value of the benefits to which these contributions entitle him or his family. In addition to social insurance, federal social security legislation provides for outright public assistance to certain categories of individuals.

The categories of eligibility for public assistance also have the flavor of social insurance: take care of people who have had bad breaks—they could have happened to you. On the other hand, the categories carefully exclude those who, in society's view, can and should take care of themselves and their dependents. Eligible categories are the blind, the disabled, the aged, and the guardians of "dependent children." The definition of "dependent children" is complicated, but essentially they are children without an able-bodied employable father in the home.

Social Insurance. Let us consider the contributory, insurance-type programs first. These are federal old-age survivors', disability, and health insurance (OASDHI) and unemployment compensation, financed by federal taxes but administered by the states. Benefits under these programs account for almost 60 percent of the nearly $50 billion in transfers I noted at the beginning, $28 billion in 1967 compared with $3 billion in 1950.

I suppose that the basic questions of political economy with respect to social insurance are these: Why should government be in the business of insuring people against these hazards? Is there not a presumption that private enterprise will respond to whatever demand there genuinely is for such insurance? Why should there not be strict correspondence between individual contributions and the actuarial value of benefits? Finally and most important, why should the state's power to tax be used to compel participation in an insurance system?

Questions like these occur naturally to an economist who like myself begins with the presumptions that people know individually what is good for them and that the best indicator of the value of a service is what people individually are willing to pay for it. My differences from some other economists are that I do not assume that we should always end with the presumptions with which we begin. It is true, at least at first glance, that the standard free-market argument seems to run counter to social insurance. Perhaps the first rejoinder should be: so much the worse for the free-market argument. For it is hard to see how anyone who has observed America before and after 1936 can close his eyes to the vast improvement the national system of social insurance has accomplished.

Compulsory saving for old age and compulsory insurance against unemployment, illness, disability, and death do undeniably involve an element of paternalism: you are forced to be prudent whether you wish to be or not. (The degree of coercion should not be exaggerated; people can curtail other provisions they might make for the same purposes.) The usual justification for paternalism can be offered without too much apology: experience shows that, *ex post*, even the initially reluctant will be glad they were compelled to participate.

But there is a stronger argument. Society is not in fact prepared to let individuals in sickness or old age, or their surviving dependents, suffer the consequences of their own imprudence. We will not let people die in the streets just because they or their parents did not have the foresight to save money for medical bills or buy hospital insurance. We will not let old people starve even if their poverty reflects their own lack of thrift and foresight. Having made such commitments, society stands to share in losses for which an individual has made no provision. Therefore society has the right to compel the individual to make the provision. The principle is the same as the one that underlies state requirements for liability insurance or equivalent evidence of financial provision for damage to others in automobile accidents.

I believe that this principle should be applied to medical care for persons of all ages, young as well as old. This is the most important unfinished business of social insurance. Everyone would be required to insure himself and his dependents against medical expenses, up to nationally specified standards of coverage. The government would offer, through the established social security mechanism, a policy with this minimum coverage. Anyone wishing greater coverage could, as now, buy supplementary private medical insurance. This arrangement would have important advantages in the provision and financing of medical and hospital care for the poor and the "medically indigent." It would take doctors, hospitals, and public health officers out of the business of public assistance, income redistribution, and private taxation. It would enable them to provide and charge for medical services on the same basis for all patients, regardless of their economic resources. Poor patients would be insured like everyone else; the scale of the financial assistance they receive from the state would take into account the costs of buying health insurance required of all citizens.

An important issue with respect to compulsory health insurance is whether individuals should be allowed to substitute private policies of equivalent coverage for the government's insurance. Suppose the contributions to the government system are set so that the system will break even if it applies to the entire population or to a representative subset. If individuals are allowed to opt out, it will be the congenitally healthier individuals who do so; they are the ones whom private insurers will take at a rate below the government's. By this process the government would be left with the worse risks—and possibly also with fewer economies of scale—and would either have to raise premiums or subsidize the public health insurance fund from general tax revenues. Either way, the less healthy would pay more in premiums plus general taxes, and the more healthy less, than if withdrawal from the public scheme were prohibited. The burden which withdrawal of their healthy compatriots would impose on the less healthy would be particularly severe if the public system were required to break even.

One's attitude toward this distributive problem will depend on how he views variations among individuals in probable need for medical care. If these variations simply reflect drawings from a lottery at birth, then those who were lucky in the drawing have no right to the economic benefit of low medical bills on top of the other advantages of good health. On this basis, everyone should pay the same premium even though we already know which ones are poorer medical risks than others. Against this view is the possibility that needs of individuals for medical care will be affected by what they have to pay for it—the possibility that they will behave more recklessly if they know that treatment is free. On this basis, people who require more medical services should pay more. Perhaps the pragmatic compromise is to include in a compulsory government policy protection only against medical "catastrophes"—relatively serious or prolonged illnesses or injuries whose incidence we can be sure is not sensitive to treatment costs.

In the case of old age and survivors' insurance, maximum contributions and benefits have now reached a level where compulsory participation is hard to justify on the "minimal financial responsibility principle" set forth above. The problem is that insurance and income redistribution are so entangled in the present system that it would be almost impossible to separate them. The situation is also complicated by the fact that the system is still in its start-up phase; current beneficiaries do not have full lifetimes of contributions behind them. But when the system reaches its "steady state" some participants will be paying in contributions more than the actuarial value of their prospective benefits. Others— those with meager histories of wages in covered employment—will be paying less than the value of their benefits.

The main reason for these discrepancies is that we

have found the social security system a convenient budgetary vehicle for giving income assistance. It is easier to finance assistance by payroll taxes outside the administrative federal budget than by general revenues. Given the reluctance of the nation to face squarely its obligations for income assistance to the poor, this procedure has some pragmatic merit. But the OASDHI payroll tax is not the ideal way to raise revenues for redistributive purposes. Property income, and wages and salaries in excess of the maximum annual amounts subject to the tax, escape the payroll tax altogether.

Moreover, the implicit subsidy involved in paying benefits to those whose contributions were actuarially insufficient may go to beneficiaries who do not need it. Wealth and property income, including private pensions and retirement benefits, are not considered in determining the amounts of OASDHI benefits to which an individual is entitled—a dispensation that is entirely appropriate for social insurance benefits but not for receipts of assistance financed from other people's taxes.

One should be cautious in suggesting changes in a working system that has served the nation well. But I think that the foregoing remarks indicate how the direction of the future development of the system might be changed.

First, we could freeze compulsory contributions and the corresponding benefits at the levels now legislated. Second, we could offer individuals the voluntary option of purchasing (by extra payroll taxes of their own or by contributions from their employers) additional packages of benefits on a strictly actuarial basis. This option would exploit the administrative economies of the federal system: collection via payroll deduction and consolidation of major parts of an individual's retirement, health, and survivors' insurance in a single account. Third, further income assistance and redistribution could be done explicitly outside the social insurance system, where it belongs. If this is not possible, then the second best approach is to finance from general tax revenues, rather than from payroll taxes, any further increases in the subsidy component of OASI benefits.

So far, I have not referred to one frequent complaint about OASDHI, namely that it is a compulsory redistribution from young to old. This is true, at least in the trivial sense that the money to pay current benefits comes in large part from the payroll taxes of future beneficiaries. In any insurance operation there is a "redistribution" from premium payers to beneficiaries. The young can have no complaint about the use of their contributions to pay benefits to their elders provided they will be similarly treated by their children. And so on, ad infinitum—unless the world collapses and cuts off a whole generation of payroll taxpayers before they live to enjoy the benefits they thought they were purchasing. If so, they will have in effect paid for the benefits of the first generation of beneficiaries, and probably no generation could be more deserving of a free ride than the one whose economic life was damaged by the depression.

Why is government in the insurance business? In the case of unemployment, the answer is clear: it is not an insurable risk for a private insurer. The reason is that the individuals insured are not independent enough risks. If one becomes unemployed and draws benefits there is a good chance that others will have become unemployed at the same time. Unlike private insurers, the central government can promise to pay money out even when there is massive cyclical unemployment. It can do so because, and in the last analysis only because, it has the power to print money.

The claim that old age and survivors' insurance pre-empted a market that private enterprise would otherwise have filled to the optimal degree and in the optimal manner would be more convincing if the record of private retirement plans were better. In fact these plans mushroomed *after* the inauguration of OASI, not before; evidently the appeal of many of them was that they could build on the base provided by OASI rather than from scratch.

All too often private funds have been poorly or un-imaginatively managed. The insurance industry has dragged its feet with respect to the variable annuity, making it difficult to insure against biological risks without accepting the risks of inflation. The option of providing for both retirement and old age by a combination of term insurance and mutual funds has become available only relatively recently, and still involves the individual in considerable transactions and loading costs.

Employers have generally offered retirement and pension plans designed to lock employees into their service; contributions are partially or wholly lost if the employee moves to a job elsewhere. Less than one-third of these programs is insured, and this proportion has been diminishing. Often the funds are invested in the enterprise itself, making the employee's wealth as well as his job and current income depend on the fortunes of one business firm. A well-functioning competitive market would provide individuals with a menu of alternatives with different kinds and degrees of risk and enable him to separate his employment and investment decisions. Our markets are evidently not that competitive or that well-functioning. Paradoxically it has been left to the federal government (and to an enterprising nonprofit institution that provides for the retirement of college professors like me) to supply a retirement insurance system that involves little risk, hedges against inflation, and permits the individual to change job and occupation without penalty.

Thus it is the nationally uniform governmental system, not the congeries of small private systems, that best promotes mobility of labor and effective competition in the labor market. Note also that for the same reasons it is fortunate that the Social Security Act of 1936 made OASI a federal function. Otherwise separate state systems might have interposed obstacles to mobility; and interstate competition for industry would have influenced the setting of contributory levies and benefits. This has happened with those programs—unemployment compensation and public assistance—where New Deal social legislation over-tenderly respected state sovereignty.

I turn now from the social insurance side of the social security system to the public assistance side.

Public Assistance. Public assistance cost $7.8 billion in 1966, the highest amount on record; of this the federal share was $4.3 billion and the state-local share $3.5 billion. In 1950 the total cost was $2.6 billion. Public assistance is the great failure of our welfare state, and its reform is the great challenge of the day. In order to give my exposition as positive tone as possible, I shall enumerate the principles which in my opinion should guide the reform, and mention the defects of the present system only incidentally to this enumeration.

1. *Need should be sufficient reason for assistance.* This is the central issue I raised at the beginning. If this principle is not established, many poor people will continue to fall between the various categories of acceptable need and receive no help. The two main exclusions from the present system are childless adults who are neither disabled nor old and normal American families. Families with father, mother, and children cannot be assisted with federal funds unless the father is unemployed or disabled. States and localities rarely help them even to the extent permitted by federal law, much less with their own unmatched money. Yet many able-bodied men, even when regularly employed, are unable to earn enough to support their families above the poverty line.

One neoclassical economic presumption seems to have come true. When assistance is conditional on certain behavior, it is scarcely surprising that such behavior is induced. To get Aid for Dependent Children, the mother must be—or at least appear to be—living alone with her children. The incentive is against normal families—against forming them by marriage in the first place, against holding them together once they are formed. It would be hard to imagine a more perverse and disastrous piece of social engineering, or one more contrary to American values.

2. *The amount of assistance to which an economic unit—an individual or family—is entitled should be objectively related to its income and family size and composition.* This is the way in which income taxes are assessed. There should not be administrative discretion to determine that family A gets more assistance this month to buy a teenage girl a new dress and family B more next month to buy a new refrigerator. The assistance benefit should be, given the circumstances of the family, a matter of right, not of charity. Assistance should not stigmatize the recipient or set him apart. It is no more of a disgrace to receive $1,000 from the government while your neighbor gets nothing, than to pay $1,000 less in taxes than he does.

3. *Minimal standards of assistance should be established nationwide, enough to keep an individual or family with no other resources from falling below the poverty line.* One of the scandals of the present system is that

states are permitted to pay extremely inadequate amounts, even though most of the costs are paid by the federal government. Monthly benefits per person under ADC vary from $9 in Mississippi and Alabama to more than $50 in New York. These differentials have no justification in cost-of-living differences and are surely a factor in inducing uneconomic migration to the urban north, intensifying the crisis of the cities. Indeed it seems likely that one of the reasons that southern states keep their welfare payments low is to encourage emigration.

A good case could be made for a nationally uniform benefit schedule, under an assistance program wholly financed and administered by the federal government. But unless states and localities were permitted and encouraged to supplement the federal payments, the national benefit schedule could not be set below a figure appropriate for the highest cost-of-living area. To avoid unnecessary expense, a basic federal program could be wholly federally financed, geared to the average cost-of-living for the country. Then federal assistance could be provided to states that wished to supplement it.

4. *The schedule of benefits in relation to income and wealth must provide incentives to work, to increase the earning capacity of the family, and to save for rainy days.* At present public assistance benefits are designed to make up the gap between an administratively-determined family budget and the family's own earnings. The purpose is to avoid giving away more of the taxpayers' money than is absolutely needed.

One unfortunate result is to equate earning of money with cheating; much of the administration of public assistance has degenerated from social case work into detective work to discover unreported earnings.

This means test amounts to a heavy tax on the family's earnings—with minor exceptions, a 100 percent tax. The family on public assistance is unable to improve its lot through its own efforts; yet this is often the most important thing it needs to learn. True enough, the welfare family will be better off with a job that pays more than the allowed welfare budget, but such jobs are not easy to come by.

Similarly, the rules of public assistance impose a heavy tax on savings. Recipients must virtually exhaust their savings, including any equity they may have in their homes, before qualifying for public aid. This requirement leaves a family that expects, with high probability, to be dependent on public assistance sometime in the future with little incentive to save during its more prosperous days.

Public assistance really does present an incentive problem, and those who wish from their hearts to improve the lot of the poor should face the problem as squarely as those whose main concern is to save the taxpayers' dollar. Which is the better way to provide incentive, the carrot or the stick? So far we have mainly used the stick: keep benefits low and where possible make them conditional on willingness to take a job if one is found. This approach has not succeeded in driving many welfare recipients or other poor people into good jobs, but it has succeeded in keeping them poor.

I think we must try the carrot instead. We must permit the welfare recipients to become better off by working, no matter how little or how much they earn. The 100 percent tax should be replaced by a fractional tax, surely no higher than 50 percent. Incentive features will be particularly important when assistance is made available to everyone on the basis of need, for this expansion of coverage will bring in many more potential workers.

The income guarantee, the amount paid to a family with no income of its own, should suffice to keep the family from poverty. Then as the family earns income on its own, the fractional "tax" will gradually reduce and eliminate the government's payment. But replacing a 100 percent tax with a fractional tax implies of course that the government will make some payments to families whose total income, earnings plus public assistance, exceeds the poverty line. There is no way to avoid this consequence; it follows inevitably from the incentive features of the proposal. For precisely the same reasons the income tax leaves millionaires with lots of money they don't really "need" while levying a real burden on low-paid workers.

If it were possible to divide people in advance into two groups, those who cannot and will not respond to incentives and those who can and will, then these two groups could be treated differently. The one could be given a fully adequate income guarantee and no incentive, and the other an inadequate guarantee with just enough incentive to induce enough earnings to lift take-home pay to the poverty line. But, except for some obvious cases of disability, we cannot make such distinctions. And if we misclassify people, we do them great injustice and harm. This is what has happened under the present categorical system. We have denied assistance to millions of people who, it turns out, cannot make it on their own. And we have denied incentives to millions of others who might be able to do something for themselves.

5. *Public assistance should be given in cash, freely disposable by the recipient, and not given in kind or earmarked for particular expenditures.* On this score our present system is a mixture. Some assistance to the poor is given in kind: medical care, food stamps, subsidized housing. Some is earmarked for particular payments: rent, a new appliance, furniture. Some is free cash, though caseworkers may try to offer a mixture of guidance and surveillance over its expenditure. The various forms of assistance are separately administered, with imperfect coordination.

Very little is gained, I think, by trying to control the allocation of public assistance by its beneficiaries. I do not have in mind merely the economist's traditional argument that such controls are likely to be ineffective so long as the recipients have any free cash to use at their own discretion, and to be an undesirable and inefficient interference with freedom of choice if they are tight enough to be effective. More important, perhaps, is the likelihood that such controls reinforce a demoralizing sense of dependence and incompetence. Treat people as responsible adults, and most of them will act that way. One common nightmare is that parents will spend welfare money on themselves to the neglect of their children. To this the answer surely is that society needs to protect children against parental neglect whatever the source of the parents' income, whether welfare checks or pay checks.

I have already discussed the problem of medical care and suggested that the best solution is compulsory insurance, required of everyone rich or poor. Public assistance would then have to be generous enough to finance the purchase of the required health insurance. This change, as I observed earlier, would place these costs in the public assistance budget of governments, where they belong, and relieve the budgets of government medical departments and hospitals. The spirit of the proposal, in keeping with the general principle under discussion, is that recipients of public assistance should enter consumer markets just like everyone else. They should not be treated differently from other people, either in supermarkets or in doctors' offices.

Does the same principle apply to housing? In my opinion, yes. It would be better to use the money now spent on rent subsidies to augment public assistance payments, and let the recipients rent, or conceivably buy, housing in the open market like everyone else. When housing carries below-market rents, then it has to be rationed, with the help of income limitations and other tests of need. These rationing devices tend to promote undesirable concentrations of low-income families in housing "projects"; to diminish incentive for additional earnings that may entail eviction from rent-subsidized space; or to continue an unjustified subsidy if they do not.

It is interesting to speculate why our society is so much more interested in providing "low-income" housing than low-income food or clothing or just low-income income. Why do we particularly like our assistance to the poor to take the form of housing? One reason, perhaps, is that we feel that the quality of housing sets the whole style of life, that people placed in good housing will live up to it in all respects, that people who live in bad housing whether by choice or necessity have a less wholesome mode of life. Experience suggests that the observed correlation must be skeptically interpreted. If successful people with stable families, clean habits, and well-behaved children live in nice houses, that does not prove that model housing will make model people.

Another reason for the preoccupation with housing may be sought in the possible effects of housing, good or bad, on people other than its occupants. One man's housing may endanger his neighbor's health, obstruct his view, increase his fire risks, or offend his taste. That is why we have building codes, sanitary regulations, and zoning ordinances. What is not clear is why these "external effects" lead us to make special effort to distribute housing more equally than we are willing to distribute income. An unsympathetic observer might conclude that perhaps we really want to conceal the poverty in our midst behind attractive modern facades.

In recommending conversion of housing subsidies into generalized cash assistance, I do not mean to say that the government has no role to play in the housing market. The market has not functioned very well, and there is much to do. Racial discrimination must be eradicated; it is not only a moral evil but a factor in increasing the rents that many of the urban poor must pay. Special efforts are needed to augment the supply of housing at low market-clearing rents. Government policy has fostered middle- and upper-class owner-occupied housing by tax advantages and interest subsidies. The pervasive institution of the amortized mortgage has made home ownership accessible to many, but restricts the financial advantages to those who are affluent enough to save as well as to pay interest. The government should, through its own efforts and those of private enterprise, so increase the supply of modest urban rental housing that market rents fall of their own weight and other rationing devices become unnecessary. To this it may be objected that the costs of building and operating such housing are just too high to be covered by rents that low-income people can afford. If so, then our poverty-line income estimates have understated the true costs of a decent standard of life by failing to include an adequate allowance for housing, and we need to scale up our concept of an adequate income guarantee.

6. *Government income transfers should narrow but not reverse differences in economic status between individuals.* This is what the personal income tax does: If Jones makes more than Smith before taxes, he will still have more than Smith after taxes, but not as much more. The government's taxes and transfers are intended to diminish inequality, but not to alter the economic rankings that emerge from competition in the market. I think that this principle is widely accepted. Mr. Superior has a real grievance if, having worked harder and more skillfully than his neighbor, Mr. Inferior, he finds the government stepping in to make Inferior as well off as he is, or better off. Superior has a much less generally acceptable gripe if he observes that, although his lazier or less able neighbor has been helped, he, Superior, still has a perceptibly higher standard of life.

In our present fragmented and categorical system, order reversals can easily occur. People in eligible categories are moved above people who are ineligible for any assistance. People in generous states and localities are moved above people elsewhere. People who just meet the income test for public housing are moved above people whose incomes are slightly too high to meet the test. When public assistance, housing subsidy programs, medicaid, and the Internal Revenue Service all administer different income tests to determine how much to pay to or take from a family—and especially when the administrations of these programs do not communicate with each other—then there is considerable scope for accidental inequities (and for "notch" situations in which a few dollars of income take an individual across a threshold and lose him hundreds of dollars in benefits or taxes). If the principles I have outlined are followed, accidents of this type will not happen.

The six principles add up to a national system of income guarantees geared to family size and composition, with benefits reduced by a fractional "tax" on the other income of the family or individual. This system must be meshed with the federal personal income tax, to provide a smooth transition as income rises between benefit-receiving and tax-paying status, and to handle rationally the numerous cases who will be moving back and forth from one status to the other.

Elsewhere, I have, with the collaboration of two Yale colleagues,[1] examined in detail the technical provisions, administrative mechanics, and costs of a "negative income tax" plan of this kind. I will not go into these details here. Suffice it to say that it is entirely feasible and that a reasonably adequate income guarantee with a tax rate of 50 percent would have a net budgetary cost—i.e., impose a net burden on federal taxpayers—of roughly $20 to $25 billion a year. This figure does not allow for savings that might be realized if the incentives offered by the plan worked as expected—or for savings from using a more inclusive concept of "taxable" income than the one used in the regular income tax. On the other hand, it does not allow fully for the costs of including in cash allowances adequate provisions for paying full economic costs of decent housing and medical care.

Twenty to twenty-five billion dollars may seem to be a large sum but it should be viewed in perspective. It is less than the annual cost of the Vietnam war. It is less than the normal annual increment of real gross national product, and about equal to the normal annual increment in real personal disposable income. It is also roughly equal to the tax revenues lost, on the current tax base, by the tax cuts of 1964-65. The sum of all deficiencies of income relative to the official definition of poverty is about $11 billion. Under the proposed plan it would take about twice that amount to guarantee everyone incomes at or above the poverty line. The extra amount is the cost of doing the job in a manner that preserves both incentives and equity. At the same time it would improve the well-being of many people who are very close to the poverty line.

The question is not whether America can afford a program of this kind but whether we have enough compassion and foresight to want to afford it. I shall conclude with some nonprofessional remarks on this subject. Inequality of income and wealth is in the last analysis more a political and moral issue than an economic one.

Americans like to think of their country as one of

equality of opportunity. The "fair race" image is indicative of a general feeling that losers have no right to claim any of the winners' spoils, that it is from charity and not from obligation that winners might share their gains. Those who trained hard for the race, and ran hard to win it, are not impressed with the claims of those who, in their view, put out less effort.

Few Americans like to face squarely the obvious facts that economic opportunity is not equal, that the race really is not fair. Even if the contestants all started even, their relative success would depend on individual genetic differences; and there is no obvious justice in letting these biological endowments determine differences in economic reward. But leaving that observation to one side for the moral philosophers, we confront the fact that the contestants do not start even. They start with vast differences in inherited wealth, home environment, educational opportunity, and social status—differences which tend to have a cumulative impact. It is only too apparent that inequality of economic condition among parents begets inequality of educational and economic opportunity among children. Even so, as is often pointed out with anecdotal example, America imposes no handicaps that cannot be overcome by sufficiently gifted and determined individuals. We can take pride in that fact and in the many examples of social and occupational mobility that attest to it. But this is far from what is meant by equality of opportunity. The exceptions prove the rule—the probabilities of success are very different for children born into different circumstances.

Since the race is not really fair, we cannot in good conscience turn our backs on the poor. It is just not true that they had the same opportunities we had but wasted them. Consequently, we do have an obligation, beyond charity—to them, and especially to their children.

Politically, there are limits on the degree of inequality consistent with the stability of a society, especially a society where peace and order depend on consent rather than on coercion. There are limits to the contrasts of poverty and affluence that people will tolerate when they believe the credo of a society that proclaims that all men are equal and that none are prescribed by birth to low status or high. Today there is reason to believe that this country has transgressed those limits—not so much because economic inequality has become greater as because the inequality we have had right along clashes so patently with the new sense of human equality that the Negro civil rights movement has brought to America.

Although every important reform movement in U. S. history has involved an assault on wealth and privilege, American politics has steered fairly clear of this issue since the early New Deal. Ever since the second world war, both major parties have consistently followed the line that growth in the total economic pie would solve all our problems, and no one would need to worry about how the pie was divided. This neutralization of the issue of income distribution had great advantages. The bitter ideological battles that dominated American domestic politics for almost three decades and kept the American business and financial community alienated from government, especially from Democratic administrations, gave way to a broader consensus and a more pragmatic approach. To this development must be given some of the credit for the acceptance of more rational fiscal and monetary policies for economic stabilization. But it is noteworthy that the tax legislation that implemented the "new economics" was not progressive in its distributional impact, and that even the cautious tax reforms proposed by Democratic Presidents have been ignored by Democratic Congresses.

The Johnson Administration has been careful not to escalate its war on poverty to the point where any taxpayer might feel that this particular war was costing him higher taxes. Once again, of course, the idea was not to jeopardize the fragile consensus supporting the Great Society. The hope was that a gradually expanding campaign against poverty could be painlessly financed from the growing yield of existing tax rates. This prospect was destroyed by the Vietnam war, a cause for which the government does have the courage to increase expenditures and, the executive branch at least, to raise taxes. As for the cautious strategy in the other war, it is not clear that it preserved the taxpayers' consensus; but it is clear that it exhausted the patience of many of those the programs were designed to help.

We are finding out now that growth in the size of the pie doesn't solve all the problems after all; maybe growth is necessary but not sufficient. Anyway, how the pie is divided is important too, and the issue of inequality was too long off the agenda of American politics. It is high time—let us hope it is not too late—to take drastic action to reduce economic inequality. I hope that affluent middle-class Americans and their leaders have enough political maturity and perspective to take such action even though they have to tax themselves to finance it.

SECOND LECTURE

W. ALLEN WALLIS

CAUSES OF THE WELFARE EXPLOSION

Remarkable as is the speed at which the prosperity and well-being of Americans is growing, this rate of growth is far surpassed by the rate of growth of governmental "welfare" and "antipoverty" programs.

Expenditures on social welfare programs designed to deal with individual welfare (not including such community services as city planning and urban renewal, parks, recreation, water and sewer works, and so forth) increased by 14 percent from 1964-65 to 1965-66 and by another 14 percent from 1965-66 to 1966-67. Since the second world war such expenditures have grown roughly 10 percent per year.[1]

For government spending on welfare to increase when income per capita is increasing would seem natural *if* nongovernmental spending on welfare were declining, or if inequality among families were increasing; but in each instance the facts are the opposite: private charity is increasing, and inequality is decreasing. Even if private charity were falling and inequality were rising, their rates of change would have to be very sharp indeed to offset the dramatic rise in real income per capita, which has doubled approximately every generation for at least a century.

Poverty has been diminishing rapidly by any reasonable definition of poverty except one that defines the poor as those in the lowest x percent of the income distribution. A definition of that sort—the bottom third, for example, or the bottom tenth—seems to be implicit in much public discussion of poverty. That definition, as far as I can see, has only one merit—that the growing number of people who are growing prosperous in the poverty game need not fear a reduction in the market for their services.

What then are some explanations of this paradox, that welfare expenditures are rising, perhaps even at an accelerating rate, while poverty is diminishing?

One possible reason why governmental welfare activities are increasing as poverty is declining is that because of urbanization the poor now are more dependent on governments than formerly. In a rural area there are, for example, opportunities for the poor to produce income in kind, by repairing their houses, foraging for their fuel, raising their food, or even carrying their water. In a rural and less mobile society there may be more mutual aid among relatives, friends, fellow-workers, church members, neighbors, and other groups.

Another explanation may be an increased awareness of what economists call "neighborhood effects." Just as a contagious disease is dangerous to others than the im-

mediate sufferers, or an unsightly junkyard causes dis-
pleasure to nearby residents, or a smoking chimney
bothers people besides those who own it, so poverty may
impose hardship on others than the poor. People may
fear that the poor will commit crimes, riot, vote fool-
ishly, spread disease, or otherwise be objectionable. Thus,
it may be argued that, although poverty is declining,
our awareness of its direct harm to us has grown, so we
are more willing than formerly to pay to eliminate it.
This increased liking for welfare activities is reinforced
by increased ability, as incomes rise, to pay for what
we like.

Some might argue that consciences are more refined
today, so people recognize more strongly their moral
obligations to their fellow human beings in misfortune.
Others might argue that consciences are blunter today,
so people have fewer compunctions about using force
to impose their views of charity or self-interest on
others. Either argument could help explain growth in
government welfare expenditures even when poverty is
diminishing.

The foregoing rationalizations of what has happened
—and no doubt many more could be and have been
contrived—reflect a rationalistic approach to political
economy that is more in vogue among economists than
among political scientists. Many political scientists would
analyze the situation in terms of power, and apply analyses like the foregoing to groups within the power structure rather than to the whole society.

More than half a century ago, discussing the effects
of universal suffrage in England, Dicey wrote:

> It has, in the first place, made known and called
> attention to the real or supposed wishes or wants of
> the poorer electors.
>
> It has, in the second place, increased the power of
> any well organised Parliamentary faction or group,
> which is wholly devoted to the attainment of some
> definite political or social object, whether the ob-
> ject be the passing of socialistic legislation or the
> obtaining of Parliamentary votes for women. For
> such a group may certainly come to command a
> vote in Parliament sufficient to determine which of
> the two leading parties, say, speaking broadly, of
> Conservative or Radicals, shall hold office. In such
> circumstances one of these two parties is almost
> certain to form an alliance with a faction strong
> enough to decide the result of the great party game.
> Hence it may well happen that socialists may for a
> time obtain the active aid, and to a certain extent
> the sympathy, of a great party whose members have
> no natural inclination towards socialism. This pos-
> sible tyranny of minorities is a phenomenon which
> was hardly recognized either by the statesmen or
> by the thinkers of 1860 or 1870, but it is a fact to
> which in the twentieth century no reasonable man
> can shut his eyes.
>
> The course of events, in the third place, and above
> all the competition for office which is the bane of
> the party system, have at last revealed to the elec-
> torate the extent of their power, and has taught
> them that political authority can easily be used for
> the immediate advantage, not of the country, but
> of a class. Collectivism or socialism promises un-

limited benefits to the poor. Voters who are poor, naturally enough adopt some form of socialism.[2]

Certainly any serious attempt to analyze contemporary American welfare measures must concentrate on politics. A major part of the explanation for the welfare explosion of the past four years surely lies in the directions pointed out by Dicey 54 years ago. During the 1950s Negro citizens began to vote in appreciable numbers for the first time since the 1870s. The two civil rights bills of the Eisenhower Administration, though their provisions regarding voting were seriously weakened in Congress before the bill was enacted,[3] nevertheless were followed by a rapid increase in the proportion of southern Negroes voting. An even more important factor in the enfranchisement of Negroes was their large migration to the north, which began during the second world war. In the north they encountered fewer obstacles to voting and soon became one of the blocs with which northern politicians reckoned in considering how hard to press for civil rights legislation—first within the northern states, then in Congress.

With Negroes enfranchised to a significant and growing degree and prepared to vote as a bloc on measures supposed to benefit Negroes (as the "poor," the "disadvantaged," "minority groups," or whatever term might be used), the political forces described by Dicey have operated strongly.

Dicey's suggestion that welfare measures result from

the votes of the poor may not have been correct for the
United States before the recent enfranchisement of
Negroes. Most of the welfare measures enacted in the
past—and some serious students of the subject say *all*
such programs—have the actual effects of injuring the
poor but helping the middle classes. Thus, the farm program helps land owners, not farm laborers or tenant
farmers; the minimum wage law helps skilled labor, but
hurts unskilled labor; social security pensions benefit
whites more than Negroes (because whites live longer
on the average), but cost Negroes more (because they
begin to work, and therefore to pay social security taxes,
younger and retire older); urban redevelopment has ag-
gravated the housing problem of the poor, but helped
middle- and even high-income groups.

Now it is possible, of course, that the middle class
supported these laws out of ignorance and misunderstanding, thinking that their only effect was to help the
poor and not realizing that they actually helped the
middle class. At least as plausible a possibility,[4] however,
is that support for these measures is not independent
of the fact that in practice their principal effects are to
provide benefits to the large middle class at the expense
of the poor, particularly by handicapping them in the
marketplace, and to some extent at the expense of high-
income taxpayers. Still another consideration is that, as
Milton Friedman points out in relation to public housing, "the general interest that motivated many to favor
instituting the program is diffuse and transitory. Once

the program was adopted, it was bound to be dominated by the special interest groups that it could serve." [5]

Another possible explanation of a political character for the welfare explosion of the past four years, besides the Negro enfranchisement, lies in the nature of American political parties.

There really is no such thing in our country as a national party in the sense that British, French, German, Scandinavian, Canadian, and Australian parties are national, because there is no effective party discipline here. The Democratic and Republican parties somewhat resemble the Howard Johnson, Holiday Inn, TraveLodge, and other systems of motels: They are franchise operations which license one or another group in various states, counties, and cities to use the name. Indeed, Howard Johnson has rather more control over its franchise operators than do the national Republican and Democratic parties over their local organizations; a motel would lose its franchise and the right to the name if it were to follow a policy deviating in important respects from the national policy.

A national party is not without influence on its local organizations, but its influence works mostly through offering such inducements as jobs on the public payroll, federal funds for local purposes, or consideration for constituents in their relations with federal agencies. The national party can sometimes be outbid by other individuals or organizations with more compelling inducements, especially substantial influence in local elections.

The national parties are in large measure federations of strong local organizations, and these local organizations are able, when they are sufficiently concerned, to bring about exceptions to, or even reversals in, national policies which they find offensive. The relation is not unlike that between the monarch and his barons in the days of feudalism.

The poverty programs of the past three years could strengthen the hand of the monarch at the expense of the barons. That is, they could bring about a truly national political party, capable of taking national stands and holding them against the opposition of local party "machines." Local machines are based, of course, on the ability to deliver votes. That ability is based in large part on their ability to deliver, or appear to deliver, to their voters the services those voters want. Before the first world war, it is said, the "boss" in a poor district ("poor" then meant "immigrant") kept track of his constituents' problems. When they were unemployed, he saw that they got a sack of potatoes. When one of the children got into trouble with the truant officer, he saw that the matter was minimized. When a scholarship was awarded by a public university, he visited the family to deliver the good tidings and the first congratulations. In short, he rendered useful personal services to his constituents, and they heeded his advice about voting.

The poverty program has brought about a great opportunity to create for the first time a truly national party, independent of local party bosses. Its programs are being administered—or, to put it another way, its large number of well-paid positions are being filled— by a national organization controlled in Washington rather than by officials of local governments or local party organizations. Correspondingly, its benefits are being conferred directly on the poor through organizations reporting to Washington, not through organizations controlled by the local political apparatus. Thus, it is delivering the services that should win the gratitude of the voters. The implications of this are not lost on local politicians. Hence the "war on poverty" has been accompanied by a noisy and bitter war among politicians in almost every city, with the local "bosses" arrayed against what they consider "usurpers" backed by Washington.

Doubtless all the forces and tendencies so far described have played roles of varying magnitudes in one or another welfare program. No one of them is the key to understanding all programs. Doubtless, too, there are welfare programs that have not been influenced in any significant degree by any of the forces I have described.

I propose to devote most of the rest of this essay to another force, one which I shall call *political entrepreneurship*.[6] I do not think that political entrepreneurship is the full explanation of government welfare activities, or that it plays a role in all of them. I do think that it is an important factor in many programs, and that some of the phenomena associated with it are interesting and important.

Politicians, I suggest, do not simply respond to needs and desires expressed by voters, weighing the support to be gained or lost by advancing one cause or another. They do that, of course, just as businessmen do it in deciding which consumer demands to serve. But just as business entrepreneurs also seek new products and services that will please consumers, even though consumers have not thought of the products themselves and therefore are not actively seeking them, so political entrepreneurs actively seek new programs to put before the public, even though no appreciable part of the public is demanding them.

Unlike the businessman, however, the politician almost never can introduce a truly new program. The businessman who is convinced that the public will find electric forks desirable in conjunction with electric carving knives does not have to persuade the public of the merits of electric forks in order to be allowed to offer them. If he believes in electric forks, he makes the investment to produce and distribute them. Then, by demonstrations, advertising, or free samples, he directs attention to the forks. People who thought the idea was silly—as many thought silly the idea of an electric knife, an electric toothbrush, an electric can opener, an electric blanket, an electric razor, an electric pencil sharpener, an electric wastebasket, or an electric letter opener—may, in fact, find merit in an electric fork when they actually try one, just as many have with the other gadgets I mentioned. If they do find merit in the new product, *they* are better off because of the entrepreneur's innovation, and *he* is better off because of his profits from their patronage. If the public does not buy the gadget, the public has lost nothing, but the entrepreneur has lost his investment—and probably his job.

The political entrepreneur cannot bring his constituents a truly new program because he has to persuade them before he can give them a demonstration. He has to persuade his clients to take the risk that a business entrepreneur would take. If what the political entrepreneur offers is something that his constituents have not experienced before, it is exceedingly hard to convince a sufficient number to agree to assigning government money to the project. Thus, for the business entrepreneur the test of a new product is not whether the public is actively seeking it but whether, when it is actually introduced, the public will prize it enough to confer their support on the man or firm who made the innovation. For the political entrepreneur, the test is whether the proposal sounds attractive enough *in advance* to win the public's support for the man or party who proposes the innovation.

Now the kind of innovation that meets the test of the political entrepreneur usually is not one that promises the voters a new service with which they are unfamiliar, but one which brings them a service with which they are already familiar. The innovations of political entrepreneurs consist, therefore, not in new services to the public, but in large part of offers to have the government pay costs that the voters are now paying personally for existing services.

The government's assumption of responsibility for education in the nineteenth century seems to have been a good example of the way in which a government welfare program may simply transfer costs from an individual to a collective basis without increasing appreciably the amount of the service. This was true both in England and the United States.

In 1833, when the government of England first began to subsidize schools, at least two-thirds of the youth of the working class were literate, and the school population had doubled in a decade—although until then the government had deliberately hindered the spread of literacy to the "lower orders" because it feared the consequences of printed propaganda. By the time of the Education Act of 1870, which first introduced freedom from fees and compulsion to attend, nearly all young people were literate. This literacy had been obtained mostly in schools which charged fees. James Mill wrote in 1813:

> From observation and inquiry assiduously directed to that object, we can ourselves speak decidedly as to the rapid progress which the love of education is making among the lower orders in England. Even around London, in a circle of fifty miles radius, which is far from the most instructed and virtuous part of the kingdom, there is hardly a village that has not something of a school; and not many children of either sex who are not taught more or less, reading and writing. We have met with families in

which, for weeks together, not an article of sustenance but potatoes had been used; yet for every child the hard-earned sum was provided to send them to school.

Thus, public education in England affords an illustration of government welfare services which did not result in new or improved services, but simply transferred the cost from individuals to the government. In England, since the tax system was regressive, there were not even the benefits of redistributing the costs to those best able to pay.[7]

It seems to have been true in the United States also that the government began to provide "free" schooling only after schooling had become nearly universal.

In New York, a commission appointed in 1811 to consider establishing Common Schools found that schooling was already widespread except in thinly populated areas. "In populous cities, and the parts of the country thickly settled," the commission reported, "schools are generally established by individual exertion." The commission recommended state subsidies to schools, but curiously—curiously, that is, if one thinks in terms of needs for public assistance and not in terms of votes—granted the subsidies uniformly on a per capita basis, rather than giving special help to sparsely populated areas.

By 1821, schooling was all but universal—90 percent of all children between five and 16 years of age were in school. While the schools were now subsidized, education was free only to those who could not afford to pay.

Not until 1867 was schooling made free, and not until 1874 was it made compulsory. Both of these steps were taken at the instigation of teachers, not parents.[8]

Another example of a welfare measure whose principal effect has been to transfer costs from individuals to the government, rather than to bring new services that people were not previously receiving, is the recent federal program to provide medical care for the elderly.

After the passage of the medicare bill and as its effective date approached, a state of near panic began to afflict many hospital administrators. Nightmares were conjured up of hordes of the elderly besieging hospitals, far beyond their capacity. That nothing of the kind would occur could have been foreseen from several studies made in the 1950s of the number of older people needing but not receiving medical care.

Perhaps the best of these studies was the one done in 1957 by the National Opinion Research Center at the University of Chicago. It found that:

> About one person in twenty in the older population [aged 65 years or older] reported that he was doing without needed medical care because he lacked money for such care. . . .

> In general, the "very sick" group in the older population seemed the least able to pay for medical care. Many of these persons were already receiving substantial free care and services.[9]

This study was consistent with several others showing

that surprisingly few of the elderly lacked medical care for financial reasons. So medicare's removal of financial barriers should not have been expected to create a sudden rush. In time, no doubt, the fact that medical care is nearly free will, as with all commodities and services, change people's notions of how much they need—contrast the amounts of water people "need" when it is essentially free with their need when it is expensive in money or effort.

It is interesting to note that when medicaid was enacted a considerable majority of the population already had private health insurance. By the end of 1959 the proportion for civilians was 72 percent and growing rapidly, having almost doubled in the preceding decade and quadrupled in the preceding 15 years.[10]

The task of the political entrepreneur, then, is to identify services which are being purchased by substantial and identifiable blocs of his electorate and to devise means by which the cost of these services will be transferred to the public. Successful innovation lies not in getting something done that was not being done before, but in transferring the costs to the public at large. Only if fairly large numbers of voters are already paying for the service will the offer to relieve them of the cost be likely to influence their votes.

CONSEQUENCES OF POLITICAL ENTREPRENEURSHIP

While relieving the beneficiary of a service of its cost will ordinarily be welcome, most of the other consequences of political entrepreneurship are likely to be less welcome.

Among the consequences are that genuine hardship cases—people who are helpless, who have no one at all to whom they can turn, who are therefore utterly dependent on social welfare—may be neglected. These people, the desperately poor, usually are not sufficiently numerous to carry influence through their own votes, and they do not purchase the services for which the political entrepreneur offers to have the government pay the bills. While they can share in these services once the government assumes the bill, such services usually are not the ones they need the most. Political entrepreneurs, for example, do not—at least they do not yet—bid for votes by offering to have the government pay family food bills. (Government programs of food distribution are, for the most part, undertaken for the benefit of food producers.)

Appalachia, and "hill-billy" country in general, was a case in point—at least until the lightning of Washington's attention happened to strike it a few years ago.

A responsible group of physicians who recently visited Mississippi reported (and in reasonably calm language, considering the substance of the report) seeing children literally starving: drinking contaminated water; eating one meal a day, and that meal inadequate in vitamins, minerals, and proteins; suffering from chronic sores and chronic diarrhea; and receiving nothing from the government or from anyone else. "Malnutrition is not quite what we found," they remarked, "the boys and girls we saw were hungry—weak, in pain, sick; their lives are being shortened; they are, in fact, visibly and predictably losing their health, their energy, their spirits. They are suffering from hunger and disease and directly or indirectly they are dying from them—which is exactly what 'starvation' means." [11]

"Our antipoverty programs have bypassed the rural poor. Rural poverty is not as apparent as urban poverty. The rural poor, especially the white rural poor, are not well organized, and have few spokesmen for bringing the nation's attention to their problems. . . . Rural people have been shortchanged in public programs. . . ." [12] I would add to that that Indians have been shortchanged too. George Wallace, the former governor of Alabama, is reported to have taken satisfaction in pointing out, when questioned at the University of Minnesota in 1964 about the poverty of Negroes in his state, that he had never seen Negroes in Alabama in as dire poverty as the Indians he had seen in Minnesota—adding that the condition of the Alabama Negroes is being ameliorated faster than that of the Minnesota Indians.

Even residents of the most prosperous and enlightened cities are likely to have their civic pride dampened by finding out what provision their city makes for the widows and children of policemen and firemen killed in line of duty. The kind of people who populate a city's prisons—mostly alcoholics and derelicts, not rapists, arsonists, robbers, or murderers—and the treatment they receive will further depress civic pride.[13] So will the treatment of the senile and the insane:

Comfortless, nameless, hopeless save
In the dark prospect of the yawning grave.[14]

Those who advocate having the government provide a service which people have been providing for themselves, such as education or medical care, often assume that the result will be a substantial increase in total expenditures on the service. The government, having access to compulsion, can easily obtain huge sums quickly for any purpose it chooses, and it appears far easier to obtain funds that way than through millions of individuals, each evaluating the worth of the service to himself in comparison with other uses for his limited income.

In fact, however, the consequence of the government's participating heavily in a welfare program often is a sharp deceleration in the rate of growth of total spending on the service.

Usually, of course, total expenditure continues to grow, so there is a certain amount of conjecture in determining whether it grew as fast as it would have without the government take-over. The data for personal health care in the United States after the introduction of medicare and medicaid are, however, so striking as to verge on the incredible. For the fiscal year 1966-67, total per capita expenditures (public and private), measured in constant dollars, failed for the first time since the depth of the Great Depression, 35 years ago, to register an appreciable gain. Public expenditures made their biggest recorded jump by far, nearly 50 percent or about $4 billion. Private expenditures fell by $3.3 billion, although they had been doubling (in current dollars) approximately every decade for the previous 30 years (a 7 percent annual rate of growth). The total in current dollars increased just enough to match the increases in population and prices, so that the per capita total, in constant dollars, showed essentially no increase. The previous year there was a rise of about 5 percent, a rate fairly typical of the past decade or longer.[15]

For education, E. G. West gives data and analyses suggesting strongly that growth in total expenditures, both in England and New York, was substantially decelerated after the government began to provide education free, and that the total amounts now being spent are considerably below what they would have been if the governments had provided only for those unable to pay.

After analyzing the experience of the National Health Service in Great Britain, D. S. Lees concludes that:

> Far from being extravagant, expenditure on NHS has been less than consumers would probably have chosen to spend in a free market. The record of hospital building in particular has been deplorable.[16]

One of the principal reasons why total spending on a service is less under a government welfare program than when individuals pay for the service themselves (the government providing only for the needy) relates to the economics of consumer choice. A second principal reason relates to the politics of collective choice.

Suppose that there is no public school system, and that each family has one child in school and is paying tuition of $500 per year. Now suppose a public school is started. The public school charges no tuition, but does levy additional taxes of $500 per year on each family. Obviously the change has made no practical difference.

(More realistic assumptions—in particular, varying the number of children and hence the tuition from family to family when the school is private, and varying the amount of additional taxes from one family to another when the school becomes public—would be appropriate for some problems but are needless complications for the point being made here.)

As time goes by, however, the shift from tuition to taxation begins to make a difference. Consumer incomes rise—in the United States they double every generation. Education, also, rises in value. Both factors cause families to wish to improve the quality of their children's education, perhaps, to a level costing $600. Since the public schools are providing a $500 education, a family may consider transferring its child to a private school charging $600. This family finds, however, that it cannot make the $100 increase, but must make a $600 increase, to an expenditure level of $1,100, because it will still have to pay the $500 tax even if its child no longer attends the public school.

Small, manageable increments in expenditures on education are thus closed. All families but a few of the richest will have to leave their children in the public school. If the public school were to stand pat permanently on its $500 education, then after a long enough time a considerable number of families would be able to manage the total outlay of $1,100.

Probably, however, the public school will not have stood pat at the $500 level. Parents who desire $600 educations, but are precluded from sending their children to $600 private schools because their total cost would then be $1,100, will try to get the public school to improve its level to $600.

If a sufficient number of parents desire this, and desire it enough so that it becomes the dominating factor in their voting, some increase will be obtained. If a majority of voters desire the $100 increase *and* are prepared to make this the exclusive consideration in their voting, the full $100 increase will be obtained. Except under such extreme conditions, the increase is almost sure to be less.

Many voters who desire the increase of $100 in expenditures per pupil will, in practical politics, oppose a $100 increase in taxes. They realize that only a small part of a $100 increase in taxes will go to schools, the rest being divided among public purposes of greater interest to others.

Migration from large cities to their suburbs is in some instances motivated partly by desires to focus tax dollars more nearly the way they could be focused through consumer choice in the market. People paying taxes of a few hundred dollars in the city may move to a suburb where their taxes are five times as high, because city taxes plus tuition at a private school exceed taxes in a suburb where public schools are as good as the private ones in the city. Surburbs may even specialize: some have excellent schools, while others provide for the retired.

The services chosen by political entrepreneurs for handling by the government tend to be those on which the expenditures of individuals are rising rapidly. The successful political entrepreneur is the one who first senses what services have grown to the point where offering to have the government pay the bills will be attractive to voters. This point is likely to come after a substantial number is obtaining the service, but while expenditures on it are still growing fast enough for people to have problems in adapting their budgets. Thus, just when expenditures are growing rapidly under consumer choice, a good political entrepreneur is likely to get them transferred to the machinery of collective choice, and that machinery brings about a slowdown in the rate of growth.

If the level of government expenditures on a service falls, under the politics of collective choice, too far behind the level that would prevail under the economics of individual choice, an entire new private system may grow up.

A fascinating example of this is occurring in England, where private health insurance is growing rapidly because the services rendered by the National Health Service fall so far short of what many people want and can afford through insurance. The British United Provident Association now provides protection something like that of Blue Cross in America for hospital bills and Blue Shield for doctors' bills.[17] About 1,500,000 people are covered, and the number is growing about 10 percent per year. We may conjecture that some day enough people will be spending enough money on this service to attract the eye of an alert political entrepreneur, who will offer to have the government pay the premiums.

An interesting example in some American cities is the rapid growth of private patrol services supplementing the public police. For Minneapolis and St. Paul, one informal estimate is that at least 300 patrolmen and guards (not including private detectives and inside security staffs) from four private firms provide supplemental police services to residential and business subscribers. The public police forces number 1,400 to 1,500. Thus the private effort equals about 20 percent of the public.

In discussing the development of public schools in New York I mentioned that the instigation for making education free and compulsory came from teachers, not parents. This reflects the principle that:

    ... those individuals who work in a service which

is provided by government can afford to bring greater than average influence to bear upon government policy since their incomes will be particularly responsive to it. In contrast, the consumers, having interests which are spread over many products and services, cannot so afford to buy influence over the supply of only one of them. In particular, they will not be able to afford the information necessary to evaluate the full implications of government policy such as, for example, the true incidence of taxation necessary to pay for "free" services or the eventual effects of a "free" service upon consumer choices.[18]

Generally, as a service is taken over by the government, it is increasingly responsive to the interests of the professionals who staff it, and decreasingly responsive to the preferences of the clients. This tendency is likely to be accentuated by the present growth of unions of government employees.

Thus, while the desire to shift the cost of services may make voters responsive to offers by political entrepreneurs, subsequent developments are likely to lead to dissatisfaction with the service: there is not as much of it as the public would be willing to pay for, and it is run with major emphasis on pleasing the professionals who run it instead of pleasing the clients who use it.

SUMMARY

One of the ways politicians compete for votes is by offering to have the government provide new services. For an offer of a new service to have substantial electoral impact, the service ordinarily must be one that a large number of voters is familiar with, and in fact already use. The most effective innovations for a political entrepreneur to offer, therefore, are those whose effect is to transfer from individuals to the government the costs of services which are already in existence, not to alter appreciably the amount of the service reaching the people. There may be, to be sure, some shifting among individuals in the ultimate incidence of the cost, but these shifts are at least as likely to be to the disadvantage of the poor as to be to their advantage.

An important result of transferring a service from the economics of individual choice to the politics of collective choice is to reduce the total amount of resources devoted to the service—that is, to reduce it below what it would have been under individual choice. One reason for this is that, under collective choice, consumers ordinarily find it difficult to make small, continuous upward changes in the amounts they spend on the service, because they are not relieved of the taxes they pay for the public service when they replace it by a more expensive service. Another reason is that the public may —quite rationally—resist the tax increases necessary to support increases in the particular services they want, because they know that the increases would be spent only to a small extent on those particular services.

Other ways in which the public is likely to be disappointed in the consequences of collectivizing a service arise from the professionalization of the service, which leads to its being run according to the notions and interests of the employees, and from the deterioration in quality that results when the demands for the service outrun the funds to support it.

With the passage of time, if the amounts people would be willing to spend individually on the service greatly exceed the amounts being provided collectively, private systems may begin to flourish again. The depressing effect on individual expenditures of the taxes being paid for the collective service becomes less controlling as incomes rise or the value of the service rises. The collective service may then become a second-class service largely confined to the poor.

CONCLUSION

You may long since have begun to wonder what all this has to do with a debate on public policy concerning welfare. What I have said has the appearance, at least on the surface, of an academic discourse on some theoretical conjectures about individual choice, political entrepreneurship, and collective choice. Presumably you expected to hear my views on aid to dependent children, the farm program, relief to disaster victims, rent subsidies, school lunches, able-bodied men on relief, mental hospitals, urban redevelopment, and so on.

I suggest that if you consider the implications of what I have said—read between the lines—you will find a lot to debate. A basic implication of my remarks is to reject the whole framework in which most public discussion of welfare measures is set.

Even though it is known that public opinion data have been used in computers to help a presidential candidate decide what stands to take, the public—including Washington journalists who pride themselves on their sophistication—continues to discuss issues largely in rationalistic and philosophical terms. If a bill is introduced in Congress, and if the preamble to the bill, the speeches of its advocates, and the propaganda of the executive agencies which would administer it all say there is a dire need that is not being met, that the bill would meet the need, and that those who oppose the bill are evil enemies of the poor and selfish friends of the rich, then the whole public discussion runs in these terms. The journalists let the issues be set for them in these terms, and they write about it for the public in these terms. They treat alike those who oppose the bill because they favor its stated objectives and those who oppose the bill because they oppose its stated objectives.

My suggestion is that a very different framework—call it "realistic" if you agree with it, "cynical" if you do not—is necessary to understand the adoption, financing, and operation of welfare programs. This framework includes entrepreneurial politics, which I have emphasized here. It also includes the theory of majoritarian democracy, the operations of legislative bodies and their committees, and other aspects of "the new political science." And finally it includes many facets that I have not touched on—for example, the use of "pseudo-events" to manipulate the public opinion that will affect the calculations of political entrepreneurs.

Rejection of the old framework is, I think, bound to distress those who realize how many of their pet beliefs and methods of approach to issues of public policy will be left stranded by the rejection. So I submit that what I have said is—I won't go so far as to say that it is debatable—but at least debate material.

REBUTTALS

JAMES TOBIN

The two main papers, at least so far as I can see, are on somewhat different topics. So I suppose my function in rebuttal is to talk about Allen Wallis' paper. I wrote out what I had to say about it before I read the transcript of the session that followed his speech, partly for lack of time, partly on the grounds that I wanted to arrive at my conclusions about his speech independently. Some of my points were raised by questioners at the meeting last week. But I will repeat them in my own way.

According to Mr. Wallis, governmental welfare programs respond to no real needs and serve no real functions. Indeed they are counter-productive, and generally have consequences the opposite of their stated aims. Anyway, poverty and inequality cannot be reasons for welfare programs, because welfare spending has been expanding while poverty and inequality have been diminishing. Since welfare programs cannot be explained as a rational attempt to meet human and social needs, the explanation must be sought elsewhere. Wallis finds it in the competitive political processes of majoritarian electoral democracy. The political entrepreneur demagogically proposes that the government provide some service free or cheap—for everyone or for politically strategic groups of voters. The service is one with which the electorate is already familiar, since most of them are purchasing it from private suppliers. But once the government program has been adopted, the total supply of the service diminishes, or at least grows more slowly. One reason is that the political competition that led to the adoption of the program somehow is suspended with respect to its expansion, and the necessary taxes are not voted.

I hope that's not an unfair summary of the thesis of the Wallis talk.

Well, I certainly don't object to regarding welfare expenditures as a phenomenon whose sources and consequences are to be scientifically dissected and explained.

Doing so, Mr. Wallis is assuming the role of a detached observer from another planet or another country, an analyst of the entire economic and political scene. He is taking this stance rather than that of the economist and citizen trying to give advice to policymakers and voters. In other words, he is looking at policymakers and voters as part of the phenomena to be explained, not as people who are subject to rational persuasion as to what they ought to do.

My emphasis was rather on the latter role. I was looking at the problem from the point of view of an economist and also a citizen, trying to give advice to members of Congress, the President, and the voters of the country on this subject.

I could wish, nevertheless, that a somewhat more occasional ray of warm human concern for the less fortunate members of our society could show through Mr. Wallis' cold and indeed cynical analysis. Not that Mr. Wallis is callous. We know that he's not, of course, for he mentions with sympathy starving people in Mississippi, rural poor everywhere, Minnesota Indians, the widows and orphans of policemen and firemen, prisoners, and the senile and insane—almost everyone but urban workers, or the unemployed, or other city dwellers.

He does not tell us, however, what he proposes to do even about the cases he does mention. We are left to wonder: Will the free market solve their problems. Private charity? Or what?

Now I have a small parenthetical doctrinal footnote. It concerns this excursion of the theory of economic competition into the realm of electoral politics and political rivalry. It is a parochial, minor cavil that stems from my own background. And I think it takes nothing away from Gordon Tullock to whom Allen Wallis refers in respect to the theory of political entrepreneurship, or from Mr. Wallis himself, if I point out that Joseph A. Schumpeter presented a competitive theory of democratic politics, complete with political entrepreneurs, in his book *Capitalism, Socialism and Democracy*, 26 years ago.

But to go back to the substance of Mr. Wallis' paper. Let us first consider whether there are any important reasons other than the insatiable opportunism of political entrepreneurs and the self-interest of the relevant professionals and bureaucrats why the relief of poverty and the reduction of inequality now seem such urgent problems in spite of the unparalleled general prosperity of the country.

First, I do not believe that Mr. Wallis is entirely correct that inequality has been decreasing, or, at any rate, inequality in its critical dimensions.

Over a long period, he is, of course, correct. The two lowest quintiles have had a bigger share of family personal income before and after federal tax after the second world war than before. In some measure this improvement can be attributed to the transfer and welfare programs that we are here to discuss. But the trend in the postwar period, though difficult to discern, does not seem to be favorable. The share of the lowest quintile in the distribution of personal income after federal tax was 5.4 percent in 1951, but declined to 4.9 percent in 1962. These are Selma Goldsmith's figures and a comparable continuation beyond 1962 is not available. However, the Michigan Survey of Consumer Finances indicates a further drop of 0.3 percent in the lowest quintile's share from 1962 to 1965. It is true that inequality as measured by similar statistics for the highest quintile has diminished slightly. But the consolidation of the position of the middle classes is no solace for the poor, perhaps quite the opposite.

Second, the urbanization of poverty, which Mr. Wallis mentions, is certainly an important factor in bringing

poverty to the fore as a national social problem. For the
city dweller cash income is essential to buy even the bare
necessities of life. The pattern and the costs of city life
are geared to the prevailing standards and preferences
of the middle class: consider sanitary requirements, building codes, the reliance on telephones, the use of automobile transportation rather than mass transit. In
addition, there are strong social pressures to conform to
middle-class standards and tastes in consumption—the
clothes the children wear to school, TV, and so on.

The third thing is that relatively more people now fall
into demographic categories that are particularly vul-
nerable to poverty. Thanks to modern medicine, people
live on after they are unable to work. Also, for a complex set of reasons—some having to do with changes in
social mores regarding sex and marriage and divorce,
some having to do with the structure of welfare programs themselves, as I argued two weeks ago—there is
an increasing percentage of female-headed families.

Fourth and finally, the most important reason for the
emergence of poverty as an urgent social and political
problem surely is the Negro civil rights revolution. Mr.
Wallis touches on this, but only to note the growing importance of Negro voters for political entrepreneurs to
woo. I would emphasize the significance of the discovery,
by Negroes and whites alike, that Negroes count fully
and equally as people. As long as this was not recognized,
the society could employ a double standard in assessing
the extent of poverty and inequality. Negroes were just

not expected to be as well off as white people—any more than Indians are—and most Negroes acquiesced in this second-class level of aspiration. But events since the 1954 Supreme Court decision have completely and irrevocably destroyed the basis of this distinction. As a result, the size of the poverty problem—that is, its social-psychological and political size—dramatically increased. Mr. Wallis surely knows that the gap between aspiration and actuality typically generates the most discontent when it is diminishing, that frustration and impatience increase when the goal in view is not only just but possible. He should not find it surprising that conquest of poverty comes to occupy a place of urgency on the national agenda precisely when the society becomes rich enough to make it a feasible objective.

Mr. Wallis is correct, of course, that there is a strong relativistic component in the social definition of poverty. But it is not fair, I think, to say that it is currently being defined tautologically so that it can never be reduced or eliminated. The present official poverty income line is expressed in absolute terms—dollars per year corrected for changes in cost of living. Under this definition official statistics show a decline in the incidence of poverty even within the short lifetime of the administration's war on poverty. As for a longer time perspective, note that FDR's "one-third of a nation" has been replaced by LBJ's one-fifth of a nation. It is true that by the absolute standard implicit in Roosevelt's "one-third" the incidence of poverty today would be much less than one-fifth. But surely it would be scandalous if the society's conception of a tolerable minimum standard of living were completely unresponsive to the massive improvements in the living standards of the majority of the population.

Mr. Wallis offers the generalization that public assumption of responsibility for providing a service previously available in the private market reduces the total supply of the service to the society, at least relative to what it would have been in the absence of government intervention. Note that this observation cancels another objection to government programs frequently offered —and strongly stressed by doctrinaire advocates of free market solutions to all problems—namely, that by offering services free or below their real costs, government programs result in an inefficient over-allocation of resources to these services. In my main paper for this debate, I expressed similar concerns about retirement insurance, medical insurance, and subsidized housing and urged that the designs of these government programs seek to minimize such errors in pricing and resource allocation. I thought that here at least I might have found some common ground with Mr. Wallis.

But what about Mr. Wallis' law? It is certainly not borne out by the history of retirement insurance, where both public and private programs accelerated after the political entrepreneurship of Franklin Roosevelt put the federal government in the business in 1936. Between 1950 and 1966 OASDI benefits rose by a factor of 26, and benefits under private pension and deferred profit-sharing plans multiplied nearly ninefold. The number of beneficiaries under the federal program rose by a factor of six, and so did the number of beneficiaries of private plans.

In the case of medical insurance and medical care, limitations in the supply of hospital facilities and physicians obviously prevent the total amounts of services from expanding to meet increased demands in the short run. I will be very surprised if supply does not exhibit greater elasticity in the longer run, thanks to a combination of government efforts to overcome shortages and private responses to higher prices.

We already know that one of the impacts of the medicare and medicaid programs on the industry involved is an increase in hospital and doctors' fees. I think that is quite consistent with general economic theory. We would expect price increases as the initial impact with those increases in prices would induce in the longer run an increase in the supply. So I would not be inclined to put too much emphasis on the one-year statistics which Mr. Wallis has doubts about.

Mr. Wallis relies a great deal on the example of education. I had not understood the question of public versus private education to be within the scope of a debate on welfare programs, but let us consider his argument nevertheless. He says that in England and New York state the coverage of the population by private elementary schooling had been expanding rapidly and indeed had become almost complete before government entered the industry. If so, the subsequent deceleration in the ratio of growth of the supply of educational services might be attributed to the near-saturation of the market, rather than to governmental intervention per se. That is, the deceleration would have occurred even if education had been left entirely to private initiative.

Nor do I follow Mr. Wallis' theoretical argument for his generalization. Once again, I should have thought that making education free, not to mention making it compulsory, would increase the demand and set up very strong pressures on legislative bodies to find the revenues to supply the demand. Indeed, I can see how legitimate questions can be raised concerning the equity and allocative efficiency of financing education, especially higher education, without heavier charges on its consumers and beneficiaries. These questions involve complex assessments of the importance of external or third-party benefits of education, at its various levels, as against private benefits internalized in the incomes or utilities of the individuals educated.

Mr. Wallis ignores these matters and concentrates instead on the inability of the taxpaying parent to make small incremental adjustments in the quantity and quality of the education his child receives. To buy the child only a slightly better schooling, the parent must pay the full cost of the private school rather than just the difference in cost above the cost of educating the child in the public school. This observation ignores the fact that parents can supplement and enrich the education of their public school children outside of school hours. It ignores the fact, which Mr. Wallis himself acknowledges, that parents can and do select places of residence so as to get the combination of taxes and public education that they prefer.

Mr. Wallis' argument also overlooks the other side of his own coin. If our public school arrangements trap some parents into buying less education than they would like, they also trap others into buying more. I do not find convincing Mr. Wallis' claim that the process of collective choice necessarily results in a lesser expenditure on education than people really want. I happen to think it results in a lesser expenditure on education in many areas and categories than I really want the people to want. But that's another matter.

Mr. Wallis says that even if people want an additional $100-per-pupil expenditure on education, they will not vote the taxes because they cannot be sure that the taxes will be used for this purpose. If so, there must be other types of governmental expenditures that have political support. And it is not obvious why a package of desired expenditure increases, along with the taxes to finance them, cannot be put together and command majority coalition support.

With respect to public education, Mr. Wallis raises issues to which some of the principles I tried to set forth in my main presentation might be applied. For example, I explained why the society might justifiably compel citizens to make certain provisions for themselves, specifically to be able to take care of themselves in old age or illness lest they become charges on the society. The case for compulsory education presumably rests on similar grounds. First is the paternalistic justification. We simply do not believe that a parent makes a wise decision for his child if he chooses not to have him educated. Second is the "external effect" justification. Not just the child himself and his parents but the whole society stands to gain or lose by the literacy or illiteracy of a child. Both these arguments lose force gradually as the child moves to higher grades, and there is certainly a legitimate issue where the line should be drawn between compulsion and volition.

The next issue is whether the society should subsidize the education of children from general tax revenues or require them and their parents to bear the full costs. The arguments for compulsory education are also arguments for subsidized education. In my main paper I argued that medical insurance should be made compulsory and that the levels of income publicly guaranteed should then be large enough to permit everyone to pay the premiums. The same kind of argument applies again here. It is reinforced, I believe, by the crucial importance of education in diminishing inherited inequalities of opportunity. I believe that equality of educational opportunity means that probabilities of leaving school with certain objectively measured verbal and mathematical skills should be independent of the socio-economic background, race, and residence of the individual child. This obviously does not mean equality of expenditure per pupil but such inequality of expenditure per pupil as is necessary to compensate for environmental disadvantages.

I believe that equality of educational opportunity really means that the probabilities of leaving school, or of attaining a certain level of schooling with certain objectively-measured verbal and mathematic skills should be independent of the socio-economic background, race, and residence of the individual child. In other words, no matter where you come from, what family you are born into, or where you live, you ought to have the same chance as the guy from the other side of the tracks of learning to read to a certain level, learning arithmetic to a certain level, and so on. Otherwise, the inherited inequality of opportunity, which I discussed in my main paper, blemishes the whole economic race. If we really mean that this is a society of equality of opportunity, a commitment to education along these lines is fundamental.

Now, that obviously does not mean equality of expenditure per pupil, because we know that equality of expenditure per pupil will not bring about this result by any means. Rather, it means such reverse inequality of expenditure per pupil—not spending more per pupil in the suburbs of Scarsdale than in the ghetto of Newark, but the reverse—such inequality of expenditure per pupil as is necessary to compensate for environmental disadvantages.

A final question is whether, as Mr. Wallis evidently would propose, parents who prefer private schooling should be allowed to withdraw not only their child but his share of the cost of public education from the public school system. I do not think this proposal is entirely without merit, but it raises several issues I would like to mention. (A similar problem in respect to medical insurance was discussed in my first paper.)

First, the designation of eligible private schools that meet standards would be even more difficult than it is now, since private schooling would not only be meeting the requirement of compulsory education but also receiving tax monies. Second, it would seem to be necessary to forbid eligible private schools to discriminate in selecting pupils on account of race or religion, or to engage in religious instruction. Third, there might be a tendency for the more easily educable students to withdraw from the public system. The public schools would be left with students whom it costs more per pupil to educate to the standard of equality set forth above.

Moreover, evidence suggests that the students with more inherited advantages provide certain external effects, for the education of other pupils. If they are withdrawn, that makes even greater the cost of educating the remaining pupils who are left without the stimulus of interaction with the more gifted children.

There are also simple economies of scale in public

education. For these reasons, the amounts which could fairly be allocated to the withdrawing students would be considerably less than any superficial overall average cost per pupil.

On the other hand, the advantage of the proposal is that competition with existing public school bureaucracies might improve the product. And that might be very important. At the moment I am inclined to doubt that the advantage outweighs the cost. I remember that —like such other imperfect systems as the social security system I mentioned in my previous paper—universal public education has in the past served the country well. In spite of its many current deficiencies, we ought to be pretty cautious in advocating drastic changes on a priori grounds.

W. ALLEN WALLIS

So that Mr. Tobin and the audience will know what I think he said in his paper, I'll start with a brief summary in my own words of the points in that paper that most impressed me.

After indicating the present magnitude and the rate of explosion in transfer payments, he discusses certain aspects of the rationale for these payments. One purpose is to relieve poverty. Massive as are the transfers— from Tobin's figures it appears that transfer payments exceeded $1,250 per poor person last year— poverty has not been eliminated, he says. He does not say whether poverty has been alleviated and, if so, by how much and according to what criterion and on the basis of what comparison. A remark about "the vast improvement the national system of social insurance has accomplished" since 1936 does suggest the use of simple before-and-after comparisons on the basis of open-eyed observation.

A reason that poverty has not been eliminated is that most transfer payments go to people who are not poor, with emphasis on a social security system designed for protection against the Great Depression. This system is a mixture of insurance and dole, and most of Tobin's paper discusses social insurance and social assistance, especially the latter.

Everyone should be forced to insure himself against medical expenses—up to a certain minimum, according to one passage, and only against medical catastrophes, according to another. The government should have a monopoly on this compulsory insurance because it is better that the unhealthy be subsidized by the healthy than that they be subsidized by the rich (or, at any rate, those who contribute disproportionately to general revenues).

Insurance for old age, sickness, disability, and survivors is not for the benefit of the person named in the policy, but for the benefit of others who would be unwilling to see him suffer should misfortune strike him. Therefore such insurance should be compulsory. Compulsion is hard to justify, however, because the present level of contributions and benefits is so high.

The social security system has proved a convenient vehicle for redistributing income. Given the reluctance of the citizenry to redistribute income, this may have pragmatic merit. However, it is not a good way to redistribute income.

The social security system offers administrative economies, whereas private plans often are poorly managed, for example, by providing insufficient hedges against inflation. Also, the federal system imposes uniform national standards and does not restrict the mobility of labor.

The principal part of Tobin's paper deals with Friedman's idea of the negative income tax. Tobin suggests six criteria for a good dole, all of which the negative income tax meets:

(1) Need is a sufficient qualification, without regard to the reasons for the need.

(2) The amount of assistance is related to the amount of need as measured by income and family size.

(3) Standards are uniform throughout the country.

(4) It preserves incentives to earn.

(5) It is paid in cash, not in kind.

(6) It never inverts the economic status of two individuals.

The cost of a suitable negative income tax is estimated by Tobin as $20 to $25 billion, or roughly $500 per officially poor person averaged over children and adults.

Tobin concludes by reflecting that this is an unfair world. People are endowed unequally genetically and they do not have equal opportunities to exploit their endowments, so justice requires that the successful share their prizes with the less successful and that the sharing not be just charity. Furthermore, the degree of inequality in America today threatens political stability—not that inequality has increased, but that our tolerance of it has decreased. We must therefore no longer rely on increasing the size of the national income to help the poor, but should revive programs to redistribute income such as characterized the New Deal a third of a century ago.

So much for my summary of what I got out of Tobin's paper. This is not to imply that there are not other topics in the paper—there are—and most emphatically it is not to imply that his treatment has the bareness, the lack of subtlety, or the various other deficiencies of this summary. I admit that I have sketched his paper, but I hope I have not caricatured it.

Let me start with some of the broadest issues which Tobin raises last.

Answers to such questions as, What is equality? What is justice? and What is the relation of justice to equality? are a little beyond my grasp. I can see that Tobin's conclusions rest directly on answers to such questions, but I am afraid that his answers elude me.

Does justice mean that each individual's rewards are proportioned to his merit, provided that his merit was obtained justly? Are merits obtained justly to the extent that they are due solely to the individual's own acts and not to some fortuitous genetic endowment or to the social advantages he happens to acquire from circumstances of family?

This does seem to be implied by Tobin, yet what is an individual other than the result of certain genetically endowed biological properties and the cumulative effects of the material, social, intellectual, and moral influences that impinge on him through environmental circumstances? Some would say that in my groping I have omitted the most important component, a divine spark given by God; but if there is such a gift of God is it just that an individual should harvest its reward but unjust that he harvest the rewards of the merits he has acquired through biological and social inheritance?

What I'm getting at is that this approach seems to lead to only one conclusion, that there should be total and complete equality, for inequalities are always due to something besides the individual's own merit, unless he is his own creator and the creator of his whole environment.

The same necessity that drove supporters of monarchs to the doctrine of the divine right of kings appears to drive Tobin to a doctrine of the divine right of the poor. Just as it was intolerable for reasons of dignity and security that the rule of the monarch be derived from the consent of the governed, so it is intolerable, also for reasons of dignity and security, that the sustenance of the poor be derived from the charity of the prosperous. Even charity which the electorate has made compulsory and collective is still intolerable. It must belong to the poor by right.

Now, if people agree on what rights are and who has what rights, it is not necessary to press the matter of defining rights. But except when societies have recognized almost unanimously a single moral authority, they have not agreed on rights. Then the question of rights is always in danger of being reduced to the question of who has the capacity to make nature yield the things that are required for human existence—either the capacity to take the sustenance directly from nature or the capacity to take it from those who have taken it from nature. The weak and the starving then have meaningful rights only to the extent that the strong and prosperous choose, for reasons of their own, to recognize such rights.

Fortunately in our society charitable motives are so widespread and so deep-seated that the overwhelming majority recognize and enforce such rights. But I do not see how Mr. Tobin is going to fulfill his need for the poor to have rights independent of the charity of others.

One of Mr. Tobin's predecessors at Yale, William Graham Sumner, wrote 85 years ago, in a chapter entitled *Wherefore We Should Love One Another,* the following:

> At the very best, one of us fails in one way and another in another, if we do not fail altogether.... It may be you tomorrow, and I next day. It is the common frailty in the midst of a common peril which gives us a kind of solidarity of interest to rescue the one for whom the chances of life have turned out badly.... Men, therefore, owe to men, in the chances and perils of this life, aid and sympathy, on account of the common participation in human frailty and folly....
>
> We each owe it to the other to guarantee rights. Rights do not pertain to *results,* but only to *chances.* They pertain to the *conditions* of the struggle for existence, not to any of the results of it; to the pursuit of happiness, not to the possession of happiness.[1]

Equality of opportunity means to Tobin, as apparently it did to Sumner, that the probabilities of success are the same for all children. Presumably he is combining here two ideas that it is sometimes useful to distinguish: Opportunity in the sense of facing a set of circumstances where an individual can influence results; and capacity in the sense of having the abilities necessary to influence results when opportunities arise.

Tobin points out that the opportunities of children born in different circumstances are not equal—which is certainly true of opportunity, of capacity, or the combination. Since he concludes from this premise that we must redistribute income, I infer that he considers inequalities in the distribution of opportunity to be largely explained by inequalities in the distribution of income and vice versa. It surprises me, therefore, that Tobin gives no attention to the problem of equalizing opportunity.

Tobin concludes his paper with a plea "to take drastic action to reduce economic inequality" because, "growth in the size of the pie doesn't solve all the problems." That reasoning strikes me as curious. If the drastic action that Tobin has in mind will solve all of the problems, he neglected to assert that, much less to buttress it. I would attribute this to hasty phrasing, were it not exactly the logic of many reformers. Their logic runs: Things are not perfect, therefore adopt my reform. Early in the paper this same standard syllogism of reformers came to mind when Tobin wrote that it had been suggested that private enterprise could have filled a certain market to the optimal degree and in the optimal manner. It is as unnecessary as it is foolish to claim optimality in advocating any practical economic policy.

I wonder whether it is correct, either in economic theory or in economic history, that policies whose intent is to redistribute the pie are more effective in equalizing income than policies whose intent is to increase the size of the pie without regard to its distribution?

The most effective measures for increasing the national income have been those that extend opportunity, or to put it another way, that bring people into economic use or improve their economic effectiveness by removing barriers to geographic and occupational movement, by training them, by providing them more and better tools, by organizing them better; in short, by increasing the productivity of labor.

Correspondingly, public policies which tend to aggravate inequality also tend to lower output. One example is the minimum wage law. Another is the agricultural program. Still others are local regulations restricting or enabling private groups to restrict entry into taxi driving, carpentry, barbering, and other trades.

Still another factor which suggests that measures promoting economic growth reduce inequality is that much economic growth is achieved by mass production and efficient distribution, bringing middle- and low-income groups services which only the wealthy could afford previously. George Stigler has suggested that Sears, Roebuck and Montgomery Ward have contributed more to the welfare of farm people than all of the federal agricultural programs.[2]

Two or three times Tobin mentions that the market economy has functioned imperfectly. The only time he indicates evidence for the conclusion, the evidence appears to me faulty, and I will return to that detail. What interests me more than the slight or casual character of the evidence he will accept when it does lead to that conclusion is his reaction when he has accepted the conclusion. I realize that Tobin does not always end with the presumptions with which he begins, because he has explicitly said so himself in his paper, plain as day. But perhaps this is one case where he does adhere to his initial presumption, for he does not ask why markets are not working well when he reaches the conclusion that they are not.

My presumption is that when markets appear to work poorly, detective work will either expose some obstacle that is forcibly preventing the market from functioning well or else will show that my reason for having judged the market to function badly is that it gives too much scope to people whose tastes conflict with mine.

While I realize that Tobin does not regard me as one of those economists to whom he referred who always cling to their initial presumptions, I regret that none of his examples of market failure affords me an opportunity to demonstrate my capacity for rejecting an initial presumption in the face of evidence.

Consider, for example, the housing market, which

Tobin says has not functioned very well. He mentions racial discrimination, which is, I fear, one of those cases where the market reflects the free choices and tastes of people only too well. When I get to be dictator, race discrimination is the very first thing I will liquidate. In the meantime, however, I am against dictatorship.

I am not familiar with housing markets, but I do happen to be aware of a number of governmental influences on them which operate against Negroes and which, when I become dictator, I will on second thought liquidate before I liquidate race discrimination directly. For one thing, a landlord who keeps his building a slum will be rewarded by the federal government for doing so; whereas if he rehabilitates the building, he will be penalized by the local government. If a landlord buys a run-down slum, the Bureau of Internal Revenue will allow him to amortize his investment over a very short period so he will pay little or no income tax during that period. When his investment is fully amortized, he can sell the building, pay income tax at the capital gains rate—unless he owns other buildings whose amortization exceeds their revenue, leaving him a loss to offset even the capital gain —and then he can reinvest in another slum and sell. On the other hand, if he should resist these entice-ments of the federal government to keep the building in bad condition and should rehabilitate it, the local government would immediately raise his taxes.

Zoning laws and building codes often keep houses from working their way down the income ladder, as they get older, to successively poorer occupants, the way automobiles work their way down as they age. When zoning laws and building codes threaten to prove inadequate for this task, the federal government may solve the problem by an urban redevelopment project which demolishes the houses before they are taken over by the poor. A 50-year-old house that has had perhaps three to five owners may decline in price as the social stratum which has provided its occupants becomes more prosperous, seeks more modern styling, or shifts to the suburbs, yet still be vastly superior to a slum. Such houses could afford good housing cheaply for the poor if they were not removed from reach by government action.

The remedy for these failures of housing markets is not a larger role for the government in housing markets, but a smaller role.

Earlier I remarked that in the instance where Tobin indicates evidence for his conclusion that a market does not function well, the evidence seems to me faulty. This instance is that of private pension funds. Tobin says that they have been poorly managed, have resisted variable annuities, generally are not vested, mostly are not insured, and often are invested in the enterprise itself.

The great bulk of private retirement plans are managed by banks and insurance companies, and there is intense competition among them on the basis of full information about actual performance. The industry is the object of continuous and intensive scrutiny by the large corporations which are its principal clients and evaluation of performance can be quite objective. Tobin's charge of poor management is simply one man's opinion and I find it not plausible.

The resistance to variable annuities has come, not from the industry, but from the government. Creation of the company to which Tobin refers approvingly, the College Retirement Equities Fund, required a special act of the New York Legislature in 1952, and, incidentally, a lot of that company's energy goes to fighting the other 49 legislatures that try to keep them out of their states or handicap them. Since 1954 a number of companies have been carrying on a running battle with numerous state and federal agencies to get into variable annuities. Today over 50 life insurance companies, the largest of which is Prudential, do offer variable annuities.

Tobin says that under private pension plans, contributions are partially or wholly lost if the employee moves to a job elsewhere. The employee's own contributions are in fact always protected under private plans, though it is interesting to note that under the federal social security system the employee's own contributions may be lost under some circumstances; for example, if he shifts to a Civil Service job after less than ten years under social security. As for the employers' contributions, vesting is rapidly being incorporated into them. It was found to be present in about 95 percent of the plans in a 1965 study.[3] To be sure, vesting is usually not immediate but follows a period of employment or attainment of a certain age, or both. A motive for instituting retirement plans has been to give employees an incentive to stay with an employer. Also, vesting is sometimes rejected by unions in favor of other uses of the same cost.

As for investing private pension funds in the employing firm itself, a study of the 100 largest retirement plans in the country in 1962 showed that 29 plans did have such investments, but all had less than 20 percent of their funds invested, and all but two had less than 10 percent.[4]

Probably the most serious danger with private pension funds is one which Tobin does not mention, namely the danger of mismanagement when unions get control of the funds, which they sometimes are in a position to do because of bargaining powers conferred on them by the government. In short, evidence suggests that private pension funds are functioning well. One considerable advantage they have over social security is that they invest in common stocks. The 100 largest funds in 1964 had 45 percent so invested, which was up from 36 percent in 1960, and it is probably up as much again by 1968, in contrast to investing solely in government bonds.

Finally, I ought to say a word about the negative income tax, since this is the principal subject of Tobin's paper. While I am sympathetic and favorably disposed toward it, I am not really convinced. I am disappointed that Tobin has not helped me to clarify my mind on the issue and come to a firmer position. I accept the arguments that Tobin makes in favor of the negative income tax. The reason his paper leaves my position unchanged is that he does not present and analyze the arguments against the negative income tax. Certainly there are valid objections. It would be worthwhile, I think, to review the history of the English poor law of 1601, which was not repealed until 1834, and which did provide for direct cash relief. The law of 1834 which replaced it was a harsh law, yet it was passed at a time that is remarkable for humanitarianism. What had become so objectionable about direct cash relief that, at a time of humanitarian reform, it was replaced by so harsh a measure? Is there danger of similar objectionable developments under the negative income tax? Or, on the other hand, is there hope that it too would serve well for 233 years?

Some advocates of the negative income tax do not argue, as Tobin does, that it would be good. They admit that it would be bad but claim that it would be a great improvement over any possible alternative. This implies that it would replace existing measures, not be added to them, and is a basis for considerably smaller estimates of net cost than Tobin makes.

Milton Friedman, who proposed the negative income tax about 20 years ago, has warned against a danger, which is in line with my paper at this seminar:

> The major disadvantage of the proposed negative income tax is its political implications. It establishes a system under which taxes are imposed on some to pay subsidies to others, and presumably these others have a vote. There is always the danger that instead of being an arrangement under which the great major-

ity tax themselves willingly to help an unfortunate minority, it will be converted into one under which a majority imposes taxes for its own benefit on an unwilling minority. Because this proposal makes the process so explicit, the danger is perhaps greater than with other measures.

Friedman concludes by saying: "I see no solution to this problem except to rely on the self-restraint and good will of the electorate." I wonder whether he shouldn't have just said I see no solution to this problem, and stopped there.[5]

DISCUSSION

FIRST SESSION

HARVEY SEGAL, *Washington Post:* Professor Tobin, would you please comment on Mr. Patrick Moynihan's proposal for a family income allowance? He recently argued, among other things, that such a scheme would be politically more palatable than a negative income tax and that it would be transferring benefits to "more people."

PROFESSOR TOBIN: I would be glad to comment on that. I have done so in the pages of the *New Republic* at some length. The children's allowance scheme, as I understand it, is a proposal to give a certain amount per month or per year to every child in the country, regardless of the income or wealth position of his parents. Mr. Moynihan and other advocates have in mind, I understand, that these payments would be subject to the regular federal income tax, although that is not always entirely clear. At any rate, that is the maximum tax to which they would be subject. The amounts that Pat Moynihan has talked about are of the order of $180 per year per child. Those amounts do not begin to alleviate poverty for families with no other income. The proposal

is therefore not a serious alternative to the kind of negative income tax or guaranteed income of which I was
speaking.

But it gives me money for my children and Rockefeller for his children. You are going to recover from
those amounts only some fraction of what is given,
depending on the marginal income tax rate of the father.
In the extreme case you recover 70 percent, the top
marginal tax rate. So you are giving subsidies to people
who have no need of them by any stretch of the imagination. I think I estimated in the *New Republic* article
that over three-quarters of the amount expended in such
a program, if subject to recapture only by the normal
federal income tax, would be given to people above the
poverty line. The Moynihan proposal would cost some
$7 or $8 billion in net federal outlays. So far as I can see,
it would do nothing to solve the problem of poverty.
It might make the Congress and other people feel they
have done something when they really haven't done anything, and it would waste a lot of money.

Now, you could imagine a children's allowance program on a larger scale which would try to give enough
money per child, to meet the requirements of a family
with no other resources with one, two, three, or four
children. But in that case you are going to have to give
a very large amount per child. There is going to be a big
jump in the schedule between a childless couple, which
will get nothing under the proposal, and a family with
one child. If it is really intended as a serious antipoverty

measure rather than just a gesture, then the amount provided for that first child is really going to be substantial.

I suspect that providing aid might influence the timing of children. Even if it doesn't influence the total number of children people eventually have. I don't see we should provide that kind of incentive.

Finally I don't understand the ethics of the whole proposal. I don't see what is wrong with adults. I don't see why adults aren't people, why they shouldn't be counted in determining the needs of families for assistance. Why should assistance go just to children? I have a feeling that the proposal is really an effort to play upon the kind of ethic that says it is okay to give aid to people who have an excuse for being poor but not for people who are in need without an excuse. Children are all right because they can't help it somehow.

Maybe that is the reason why (Daniel) Moynihan and other advocates of this assistance think that the children's allowance will go through Congress more easily than other proposals I am not sure that is a good thing. I think it would be better to face the real problem more squarely.

PATRICK BOARMAN, Director of Research, House Republican Conference: You just mentioned people in need who don't have an excuse. Now, if they don't have an excuse for being in need, why should they be helped? Don't we have a lot of people in our society who would like to get a handout, who are lazy by nature and who don't like to work, as distinguished from those whose backgrounds, education, etc., have handicapped them? How do you separate out the people who want to take life easy, the goldbrickers, from those who are really in need? How do you avoid reducing some persons to a permanent life of dependency and lowering the productivity of the society?

PROFESSOR TOBIN: I wouldn't deny that there are some people who meet the description you provide, although I am not sure that there are so many. We don't really have a way of distinguishing those people from others. We cannot really judge their reasons for being in need in any Olympian judicial way, since those reasons probably go back to very deep things in their origins and past environment. That is the reason why, I think, we really have to make sure people don't starve, whether in some larger sense it is their own fault or not. What I propose is a way of doing it which also retains the incentives to which you are referring. There will be a system of getting assistance to people in need when they are in need. But the system will also make sure that people will be better off by doing something for themselves, by being self-reliant, by increasing their own earning capacity than they would be if they didn't do that.

DR. BOARMAN: Doesn't that depend on the level of payments that are made, whether they have that incentive?

PROFESSOR TOBIN: It depends partly on the level of payment but it also depends on the system of taxation or implicit taxation that is involved in the income test on the basis of which the grants are given.

Suppose it is given on the following basis "We'll make up for you the difference between some budget, whether that budget is small or large, and what you can earn for yourself." Then you are imposing essentially, a 100 percent tax on their own earnings. That is a substantial disincentive and one that no one would justify if it were proposed as a tax rate in the high income brackets. The outcries about incentives, if that kind of marginal tax rate were proposed in the positive income tax, would ring in every editorial page in the country.

Yet, that is the kind of incentive scheme that we have imposed upon the people who are dependent on public assistance. For that reason I think the basic way of avoiding your problem is to provide a fractional tax for people who are in this position.

Things would be different if we were able to distinguish ahead of time between different people. To some we could say we know that you are just loafing and so we are not going to give you any income guarantee. But we know that your neighbor is doing the best he can and that isn't very good, so we give him an income guarantee. There is no way of doing that any more than there is of saying to somebody who has the capacity to earn $100,000 and contribute it to the society that we are going to tax him a lot unless he earns that much. We don't do that because we are not really able to tell in advance whether a person has that capacity or not.

EDNA GASS, House Government Operations Committee: Dr. Tobin, you said that it was your estimate that an adequate negative income tax, or income-maintenance scheme, would cost $20 to $25 billion more than it costs us today for our present level of benefits. How much would this sum be reduced if there were an adequate scheme of old age insurance? After all, about a third of the poor are the aged and we don't want them to work. If we had a scheme of social insurance that would lift their income above the poverty line, and if we had a scheme of unemployment insurance that covered. . . . Many of the poor, after all, may have a job one week but can't get a job the second week; over the course of a year they may be out of a job for a part of the year. This then means that their incomes are very low and that they are therefore poor.

If these two categories were taken care of under principles that the American people accept, how much of the residual poverty program would there be?

PROFESSOR TOBIN: If those two categories were taken care of, that wouldn't be done cost-free. There would have to be some taxes raised.

MISS GASS: But not through a negative income tax.

PROFESSOR TOBIN: No, but through some kind of tax; I was talking about the net burden on the taxpayers altogether. So then the question becomes: Which is the more efficient way of taking care of those people? I believe that probably it is more efficient to do it by the negative income tax and the reason is this: If you raise the minimal old age survivors' insurance benefits, you are raising them for everybody who is entitled to those insurance benefits. The entitlement to those benefits has no income test other than the prohibition on work or the tax on work that applies to retired people under the age of 72. The entitlement certainly has no test which reduces benefits on the basis of income from property.

MISS GASS: I was only speaking of raising the minimum.

PROFESSOR TOBIN: I know, but even those who might qualify for the minimum may not be people who would qualify for assistance under a negative income tax plan. Under a negative income tax plan their total income, including social security and other retirement benefits, interest, dividends, and everything, would be taken into account in determining how much they are entitled to. Thus you would have a greater mechanism for pinpointing assistance to those in need than you would by a blanket rise in social security benefits. It seems true also, to a certain degree, of unemployment compensation.

I think the difference between the two kinds of programs is that one is really based on the idea that you earn rights to benefits on the basis of prior contributions, regardless of current need, while the negative income tax, like the regular income tax, is based on the circumstances at the time: income and family size and wealth. So I think the latter is the cheaper, more efficient way of meeting need for the same tax dollars. There may be different taxpayers paying because in one case you will be hitting by payroll taxes the contributors to the insurance schemes and in the other case you are hitting the general public, the general income tax payers. But, there again, I think the preference is for hitting the general income tax payers as a more equitable source of revenue.

MISS GASS: The financing of social security can be changed.

PROFESSOR TOBIN: The financing of social security could be changed, as I suggested in the talk, at least for the future by making a distinction between the assistance or the redistributive part of social security and the strict insurance part; and then by appropriating to this social security fund, from general tax revenues, amounts which would take care of additions to the subsidy assistance or the distributive parts.

But then I can't quite see the justification for doing that without imposing rather more discriminating income tests for recipients of the taxes so used than the tests now extant in the social security system. The social security system right now has very little income test in it.

HERBERT STEIN, Brookings Institution: You have been very modest in taking credit for savings that might result from the introduction of this plan. It has seemed to me that it might be possible to take credit for some general improvements in the efficiency with which the economic system operates if, once having installed such a system, we could get rid of a number of obstructions to efficiency that were introduced with the thought that they helped to do something about the poverty problem —like the minimum wage, agricultural protection, inefficient investment in Appalachia and other backward areas and, possibly, although I suspect this is a more treacherous area, the support for the power of labor unions. But, in general, it seems to me that there is a category of anti-efficiency policies which have heretofore been justified on the grounds that they do something about poverty that we could more easily dispense with if we had a thoroughgoing system for transfer of payments such as you suggest.

PROFESSOR TOBIN: I agree entirely with that. However I don't think that I would like to count those chickens before they are hatched, because I would still be in favor of this reform even if it wouldn't be able to make the savings that you just referred to.

DR. STEIN: You might feel freer to argue for them, though.

PROFESSOR TOBIN: Feel freer to argue for them, yes.

ANTHONY WEINLEIN, Building Service Employees Union: You are concerned with the question of poverty and you have proposed national health insurance plus the negative income tax. Isn't it necessary, as a very essential part of any program to take care of poverty, greatly to expand our expenditures for education, not only to take care of the future generations and to keep them out of poverty as much as possible but also to take care of present workers who are subject to periods of unemployment because of technological developments and that sort of thing? Aren't we going to have to spend much more on education, maybe as much on education as you are suggesting the negative income tax will take?

PROFESSOR TOBIN: Yes, I certainly did not mean to indicate that I was giving a recipe for the elimination of poverty, or the elimination of the causes and sources of poverty, by the reforms in the system of public assistance that I was advocating. Our subject here is the welfare system and not the whole program of the War on Poverty.

Certainly what you say is right. We are going to have to do a lot in education, in manpower training and in manpower retraining. I don't mean to say that you won't have to do these things if you do what I was advocating tonight. That is not the whole answer.

On the other hand, I think that whatever you do in the field of education, whether for children or adults, is going to take a lot of time to make a real impact. For quite a number of years it likely will still be true that a lot of people in our society will lack the capacity to earn the kind of living for themselves and their families that we regard as a tolerable standard of life. That being the case, we are going to have to have a much-improved system of assistance anyway during the time when we hope that the more fundamental measures, education in particular, have a chance to take effect.

I add to that that I think it is also advantageous to have a system of income assistance which reinforces and supplements any structural program, in the sense that it provide incentives for people to get the education, take the training, and so on, so that they will be able to make themselves and their families better off if they do so.

SIMON LAZARUS, Federal Communications Commission: I was surprised by your intimations that your system of a $3,000 a year guaranteed annual income could serve as a replacement for a public housing program. Do you believe that? Do you believe that with everyone having $3,000 a year guarantee that we would not need public housing?

PROFESSOR TOBIN: I didn't say $3,000 as a sacred figure. Perhaps I should say that if you followed my prescription for including in the basic income guarantee the costs of some of the subsidies which are now given in kind, like medical care and housing, then the guarantee would have to be somewhat larger than that in order to include those costs as well. I don't want to be stuck with any $3,000 figure on that basis. Also, I do believe that it is necessary to build more houses of a kind suitable for people with incomes in the range we are talking about to rent or to buy.

I would like to see us move to a situation in which those houses would be in sufficient supply so that their rents would be market clearing. There would be no necessity for rationing, for saying people above certain incomes can't live here. The incomes of poor people would be such that they could just choose to rent them or not. They would not have to stand in line to be allocated to them; they wouldn't have to meet different income tests for being there than they have to meet for getting general public assistance. I think that would be a better system than we have now.

MR. LAZARUS: How much more would that cost in addition to the $25 billion a year? I mean, it would cost quite a lot, would it not, because it would require an enormous transformation of the housing market.

PROFESSOR TOBIN: Wait a minute. The total amount in the federal budget for housing or community-development enterprises is something like a billion and a half dollars. The amount of housing subsidy involved now is relatively small. I don't know what it is exactly but it's not a fabulous figure.

KIRKLEY COULTER, Senate Antitrust and Monopoly Subcommitttee: To pursue that thought, then would you figure that as your proposal is phased in you would see further construction of public housing, of the types that we now have, and that you would also proceed to get rid of the present mode of operation of it on a market basis?

PROFESSOR TOBIN: We might get rid of the present mode of operation of it in the sense that it rents at below market rates and therefore rations the occupancy to the persons who meet certain tests. But I don't have any ideological opposition to having the government build and own houses and rent them in the market. I think probably local governments, with the help of our government, are better entrepreneurs for this purpose than the federal government.

Our sponsor tonight is the American Enterprise Institute and I would consider government to be included in enterprise. I don't think that there is an objection to having the government in that business to the extent that is necessary to increase the supply of houses where the market hasn't worked very well. Maybe it should be in the business. Maybe there should be more encouragement to private builders. I am in favor of that too.

The point is that I think efforts are needed to increase the building of houses of a more modest character, but not on the basis of renting them at below market rents and rationing their occupancy.

MR. COULTER: So that you are talking about renting the housing for what it will bring, in effect?

PROFESSOR TOBIN: That's right. That's right.

MR. COULTER: Which may mean raising the rents, if you can.

PROFESSOR TOBIN: Which may mean raising the rents and which will then mean giving more to the people that need general assistance, and counting this in the calculations of budget costs that go into the reckoning of how large general assistance should be.

MR. COULTER: Should they continue to be financed with tax-exempt bonds?

PROFESSOR TOBIN: You mean should there be any interest subsidy in the building of such houses?

MR. COULTER: Yes, interest subsidy and also tax exemption.

PROFESSOR TOBIN: That raises a large question about tax-exempt bonds. Tax-exempt bonds are even used for manufacturing industries all over the country. I have a general objection to tax-exempt bonds as a method of assisting state and local governments. It is an inefficient method. But I think that is a larger question, a different question.

JOSEPH MEYERS, Department of Health, Education, and Welfare: I would like to make a comment and then ask a question. I find myself in general agreement with Professor Tobin on his listing of the inadequacies of the present income-maintenance provisions of the public assistance program and of his listing of the essential criteria that he says should go into more adequate programs.

On the national minimum standard and the fact that there is this wide variation among the states: From all of the evidence that I have after working in the program for quite a few years, none leads me to conclude that low payments have as a motivation the encouragement of migration. By way of illustration, Mississippi does pay an inordinately low assistance standard. On the other hand, in terms of effort related to fiscal capacity, it rates relatively quite high, as compared to some of the other states.

On the question of cash as the preferred method: I think it might be well to point out that the only exception to that, in terms of the federal-state programs on which you can get federal participation in your payments, is in the medical field. Earmarking the cash for the refrigerator is not permitted under the existing federal system, if you want to get federal money for that payment.

On the incentive part: The recent amendments, the 1967 amendments just signed by the President on January 2, do now provide in the family program a work incentive for people who enter into the training program and get into employment. It amounts to $30 a month plus one-third of earnings over and above that. I think this is along the line you suggest as being the right way to go.

I would like also to elaborate a little more on the difference between your fourth point, which is that the schedule of payments should provide incentives to work and save, and your sixth point, about Mr. Superior having some advantage over Mr. Inferior, because it didn't quite come through to me the distinction you were making between those two points.

PROFESSOR TOBIN: Let me first comment on your comment. I think you know more, much more about the states' motivations in these matters than I possibly could. I'll take your word for it, suspicious though I am.

On the second point, I guess I don't quite understand the situation. Certainly you hear of plenty of cases where the welfare client is required not only to present a case for a particular extraordinary expenditure, but also even to get a bid for it. In effect, he has to find out how much it is going to cost and then have the expenditure approved by the case worker and the administration in order to make it. For example, in my home town there has been considerable publicity given to a contract which has been made with Sears, Roebuck for supplying refrigerators and such appliances for welfare clients, whereas in the past they have been required to shop around for used ones. It was my understanding that these were expenditures for which they had to get approval. Then there are also certainly cases in which the welfare budget of the family is dependent on the rent it has to pay, and even cases where the welfare department pays the rent directly to the landlord rather than to the client.

I thought all this was done in programs which are assisted by federal funds. But maybe I don't understand.

MR. MEYERS: Perhaps I can explain that a bit, if you want me to, before we go on to another question. The difference is between saying that the money is earmarked for that in terms of it being controlled for this as distinguished from being built up and justified because of this. A lot of states, it is true, do have what they call a general, fixed, budgeted amount that would be forthcoming on a regular monthly basis and then they have the so-called special needs—

PROFESSOR TOBIN: Yes.

MR. MEYERS: Someone comes along and says, "Well, I need a refrigerator." "How much is it going to cost?" "Well, it is going to cost $200." Then they give the individual the money for the refrigerator but, if the individual doesn't buy the refrigerator and does something else with the money, there is no penalty involved. He just doesn't have the refrigerator; but he can spend the money for anything he wishes.

I had a letter come over my desk today in which someone was complaining. A woman had been granted $50 a month for four months to buy a refrigerator. She had contracted for the refrigerator and made the first payment and then had spent the other $150 for other things instead of for the refrigerator. Couldn't we do something about it or couldn't the state do something about it? The answer is: We can't, and I think this is the point.

PROFESSOR TOBIN: You can next time, though. [Laughter.]

MR. MEYERS: Yes, you don't buy her another refrigerator.

PROFESSOR TOBIN: Or another anything, I suppose. Okay, I don't know whether that is a distinction without a difference or not.

MR. MEYERS: I think it is, in terms of your notion that it should be cash and that the person should have freedom to spend it, I think it is a distinction that is worth noting.

PROFESSOR TOBIN: All right. It violates one of my other principles, that the need should be objectively and impersonally measured.

MR. MEYERS: I agree with that.

PROFESSOR TOBIN: I certainly welcome the incentive provisions of the new legislation, which may be about the only provisions of it which should be welcomed, I guess.

I think that you are right about the principle of narrowing but not reversing income differences. Probably it follows as a corollary from the others that a system which followed the other principles would also have that one too. I like to point that out because I think there are a lot of people who find something strange or even un-American about the income guarantee and negative income tax who might be appealed to by realizing that it at least conforms to this very American principle of preserving economic rank. In contrast, the kind of variegated, ununified, different system that we have can easily not have that result.

GERALD POLLACK, Department of Commerce: Professor Tobin, you commented that there are regressive aspects in some of the welfare programs. Professor Friedman has argued that, in general, federal programs are perverse in that they achieve objectives generally contrary to their intended purposes. He has argued in the case of the social security program that the not-so-poor are benefited or subsidized, in effect, by those who are poorer than themselves.

I wonder whether you regard this as a general problem or, in any event, whether it could be said at all that those below the poverty line are contributing to the welfare of those above it?

PROFESSOR TOBIN: They certainly are in the respect that they pay a lot of excise taxes and other consumption-levied taxes which are used for purposes that assist people who are much better off than they.

I think that Christopher Green's study of transfers, negative income tax, and poverty[1] has some calculations of all tax burdens levied on the poor. It is really quite remarkable how much taxes they do pay, one way or another.

In regard to the social security system, I am not sure what the net of it would be as to direction of redistribution. I did indicate that at least it has some redistributive aspects to it. The redistributive aspects have at least some potential for being regressive, in that the taxes are payroll taxes; that is, they are not taxes on property income and they are taxes on the first X-thousand dollars of wage income, and not the remainder.

So it is quite possible that some of the subsidies of those who pay the higher amounts of contributions for a longer period of time go to people who are better off than they. But I don't know what a careful study of that net redistribution would show.

WALTER WINGO, *Nation's Business* magazine: Don't you feel that once such a system is started that it will be much like the minimum wage, an unbeatable temptation for congressmen continually to raise the level of this basic standard, the poverty level, so that there is always a large group of voters on handouts?

PROFESSOR TOBIN: I haven't noticed that political effect working yet. It hasn't worked in the direction of accepting such a program. In fact, the general politics of the country seems to be that the minority who are poor have very little political impact relative to the majority of the population who are fairly affluent.

I think the analogies you suggest really won't apply since the minimum wage has behind it not only the interests of the relatively few people, politically speaking, who are paid at the minimum wage and might hope to have it increased, but it also has behind it the perhaps misguided political interest of a large number of other workers who believe that their wages will be increased if the minimum wage is increased.

The same is true of social security. I think that the reason that the increases of social security benefits have a wide political appeal is that a vast multitude of the majority of Americans are going to benefit thereby. There aren't any restrictions as to who will benefit. The middle class is strongly for social security, and rightly so, because it is a big thing for them.

I am not sure that a program like this, in which the beneficiaries are always going to be the lowest fifth or tenth of the country, has that degree of political appeal.

DR. BOARMAN: I take it from what you have been saying that we are to regard poverty as a relative term, that today's poverty is no guide and that today's poverty may have been yesterday's affluence and that, therefore, economic growth as such is not going to solve the problem. With economic growth we may end up with the same structure of income inequality that we had at a prior period. If this is so, if we are going to have the poor always with us in that sense, and if redistribution of income is the solution to the problem, how far can a society that is basically built on a system of incentives, such as ours is, go in such redistribution before we impinge upon the mechanism that makes for economic growth in the first place?

Would you care to speculate on whether there is some cutoff point that might be reached? For example, although there are other factors operating, the British economy seems to have reached the point where there is a serious question whether they can afford the welfare that they thought they could. They have reached the point where other nations have been unwilling to forget the tab for their welfare program and have forced the devaluation of the pound. The dollar is also in trouble internationally for many other reasons besides our welfare programs. I'll grant.

But would you care to speculate on whether there is a theoretical limit to the degree to which any society can redistribute income from one part of it to the other?

PROFESSOR TOBIN: First, in regard to your observation on the fact that there is a large relativistic component in the definition of poverty, I think that is undoubtedly true. The standard that we regard as defining poverty will be in absolute terms on higher income levels ten and 20 years from now than now. I sure hope so. I think it would be pretty disgraceful for this society to continue to define what it regards as the tolerable level of life for its citizens in terms of what it meant to be poor in 1776.

But, at the same time, I suppose there will be some compromise between a purely relativistic and absolute standard, as indicated by the difference between the one-third of the nation which Roosevelt was talking about and the one-fifth of the nation that Johnson is talking about in his war on poverty. So probably economic progress will diminish the category. It won't always be the poorest one-fifth of the population. It probably will diminish. But it will probably also not be always the people who are under $3,200. It will be, in present dollars, some higher amount.

To a certain extent I think that the redefinition of absolute standards may be justified by the fact that when the rest of the society is affluent and adopts certain patterns of life which are geared to its standard of living, it is not only relatively more difficult to be poor but it costs more absolutely.

If the whole society is geared to the private automobile, then public transportation, which might be a way out for poor people, just isn't there or is very expensive if it is. So there are some problems like that which we shouldn't overlook.

I don't think that we know the answer to the large question you raise on redistribution. There are societies where the burden of welfare payments and income redistribution, and the taxes to pay for them, is larger than it is here in relative terms and societies which are continuing to show vigorous economic growth. One of the biggest welfare states in the world is West Germany and they seem to be doing all right. So is Sweden. So I doubt that we are near that kind of limit.

We have been hearing for a long time this forecast that we were going to kill the goose that lays the golden egg, if we adopt welfare programs and so on. We have heard that for at least 30 years and probably longer. It was said about the social security system when it was first put in, and I expect it will be said about every improvement in social security or about the negative income tax or anything else. Maybe some day the cry of "Wolf" will be justified, but the rate of growth of the economy doesn't indicate that it has been justified yet.

We have had, even in recent times, even in peacetime higher tax rates on income than we have at present. So I don't think we have come to any sort of tax limit. The basic sources of economic growth are the advance of technology and the supply of savings for capital formation. I don't think there is anything inconsistent between those proceeding at a high rate and a more equal distribution of income.

PAUL O'NEILL, Bureau of the Budget: I would like to ask you an operational question about compulsory health insurance. I believe you said that compulsory health insurance would overcome the scaling-of-fees problem. I think our experience probably validates that. With the medical assistance programs that we now have everyone is paying a higher rate, unfortunately. I wonder, in accepting the idea that we would like to get to the point where we can satisfy everybody's health needs, what is the horizon for an acceptable ideal income level for the people who deliver the service? Because of the way the market is structured for medical service, it is a very difficult problem to regulate the amount of money that should be extracted from the system that is a comprehensive health insurance system.

PROFESSOR TOBIN: I think that is a very good point. I guess I should have made some remarks about the industrial organization of medical care parallel to the one I made about housing. My view is that the government program in this area shouldn't be limited to providing insurance, but that we ought to work on the supply side as well as the demand. The basic reason for the problem you mention is the shortage of facilities and the shortage of doctors. There are various reasons for this, not excluding the restriction of entry into the industry. Therefore, I certainly agree that we have to work on that side of the medical-care market also.

GEORGE IDEN, Joint Economic Committee: Professor Tobin, do you hold much hope that there is any way out of the present ideological impasse, namely, that people might conceivably be for the negative income tax out of growth but not through digging deeper into the pocket?

PROFESSOR TOBIN: There may be a way out provided by time and luck. If the war in Vietnam is ended, then the budgetary situation would seem a lot easier. The prospect for reforms of this kind would be more attractive. Also we musn't forget that even if you have tax rates constant their increased yield every year at the federal level is some $7 or $8 billion. What we are talking about even for the relatively ambitious plan that I was talking about is on the order of three years of the increment of federal tax revenues at the existing rates.

But I don't want to put too much stress on that because I know that there are going to be lots of claimants for those annual increments of tax revenue and lots of claimants also for the budgetary space that is released by the end of the war, if and when that happens. Among those claimants, of course, will be the advocates of general tax reduction. So all I hope for is to get an interest in having the claims of this kind of program in there fighting with the others for the division of that pie.

KENNETH SPARKS, Office of Economic Opportunity: Professor Tobin, you have talked and commented not too unfavorably of the idea of having education and training and manpower programs conditioned to some sort of income-maintenance program. Operating at an optimum efficiency level, what do you think the aggregate tab would be for both programs in addition to the income-maintenance programs?

PROFESSOR TOBIN: I really don't know those programs well enough to say that. I have some feeling that in public school education in the cities it might take twice as much expenditure per pupil as we are making now in order to do a decent job of having real educational equality.

What we ought to mean by equality of educational opportunity is not equality of expenditure but equality of results, that is, equal probability of performing at the same level, regardless of who you are and where you came from and where you went to school. In order to achieve that sort of thing, it is obvious that we have to spend a lot more per pupil in the inner-city schools of the cities than we are spending elsewhere, instead of having the reverse pattern. So that would be quite a considerable expenditure in education.

I just don't know about the manpower training programs. My feeling there is that it is an awfully difficult thing to do and a slow process.

SECOND SESSION

WALTER GARVER, U.S. Chamber of Commerce: Mr. Wallis, I have been sitting here trying to fit your framework of political entrepreneurship into the situation we have in Maryland and some other states, where you have now a form of compulsory auto liability insurance. I am having some difficulty in seeing where this takeover is supplying something that the consumer would not like for you to sell. I have the feeling that it was sold, at least, on the rationale that this is to protect people from others who couldn't take it out.

MR. WALLIS: That didn't have a question mark on it and I guess that is a good thing, because I don't really know anything more about that than you do. I have noticed the move going on to make automobile insurance compulsory and, in effect, to require the companies to insure the uninsurable cases and to keep the rates low. But I haven't really thought about exactly how that fits into political entrepreneurship, if it does. It is obvious that it has elements of what I was talking about. Very large numbers of people are now buying automobile liability insurance. The cost is getting steeper and steeper.

Voters are probably more and more responsive to somebody who says, "We will have the government pick up
the bill."

What you are talking about isn't quite having the
government pick up the bill—yet. Some of the steps are
of a sort that would force the companies out of business,
or require government subsidies.

About all I have to say is that it seems to me there are
a great many subjects besides medical care and education
that would be interesting to examine from this point of
view. I haven't really had a chance to investigate them
carefully enough to include them here.

I would like to see a more systematic study. I expect
there would be some generalizations about what kinds of
things do and what do not fit this analysis.

One possibility might be the interstate highway system. These limited-access throughways were being built
at a very rapid rate as toll roads. Then just before the
1956 election, Congress passed the bill to build 41,000
miles of interstate highways. About half of this has been
built. It seems a pretty poor record 12 years later, that
they have only got half of it built. Maybe from a financial point of view I am glad it isn't more, but, as a
driver, I am sorry it isn't a great deal more. I don't have
any doubt that if it could be financed by the people
who want to use it, it could go faster. Those people who
want to make a trip and want to go on that kind of a
road are often willing to fork up the cost of the toll, so
that the roads could be built from their revenue. But

those very same people will scream if you try to raise taxes, because they figure the money won't go into interstate highways, it will go into controlling air pollution, which they may not be concerned about.

NORMAN TURE, National Bureau of Economic Research: On this point, where is the initiative for the public?

MR. WALLIS: It is from the White House.

MR. TURE: I am sure there is reason but what reason is there to suppose that this is not in response to substantial pressure out of the trucking industry? The trucking industry would not care for toll roads. They would much rather have somebody else picking up the bill for that, like the railroads.

MR. WALLIS: Yes. Well, to that extent it would be an example of what I am talking about. I think if the trucking industry was not interested in these toll roads, it may have been misguided. It would have gotten a lot more of these roads faster on a toll system. When you consider this particular program, eliminating the highway system wouldn't affect their taxes directly very much. But if a lot of these programs were eliminated and handled through a market arrangement, the total tax system would begin to show some effect.

If you were studying highways, it would be interesting to look at California separately. There they levy a gasoline tax which can't be used for anything but building freeways. It is a kind of toll system, except the toll isn't allocated on the basis of the use of these particular roads, it is mostly allocated on the use of city streets and so on. Nevertheless, there is a different mechanism operating there than for the interstate system, and I have the impression that freeways have been built faster in California than in the rest of the country.

ROBERT LEVINE, Office of Employment Opportunity: I have some problem with your medicare example of public spending cutting down on total demand for goods. For one thing, I don't think that the data you quoted fits well with your theory. The other thing, I have trouble with your data. Although I don't challenge your data, I would like to get further explanation on it.

MR. WALLIS: Incidentally, I don't believe the data either. Let me say I have some footnotes in the actual paper (which were not read). One of them says that I just don't believe those data could be right. It is consistent with my theory and in fact, I predicted a year ahead, to some of our medical administrators, that medicare and medicaid meant the end of the untrammeled growth of health-care expenditures in the United States. What I meant was that there would be a gradual deceleration or a leveling off. It never occurred to me, however, that expenditures would come to a screeching halt from a long, sustained, rapid rate of growth to no growth whatsoever in one year.

Frankly, I just don't believe the figures. They are official government figures but they are marked preliminary. If they are right, then I think next year there is going to be a jump, that there is some kind of an erratic factor in there. It just couldn't stop that abruptly. But it is consistent with my theory, entirely consistent with it.

MR. LEVINE: You have answered most of my question with that comment. Let me just pick up on one of the theoretical points, which I think might apply to the medical care and it might apply to things other than public education in England.

I don't think the theory works out well, if you can buy increments, relatively small increments, on top of the public supply. For example, in the medical care case, suppose I have a particular kind of disease with which I wouldn't trust a public doctor (by the way, I think that doesn't work either because there is insurance for private doctors) where I can buy a small increment, whether it is care for a particular case or tutoring for a particular kind of course in school. It would seem to me that you could add private spending on to get, say, this 600th dollar onto the first $500 without giving up your benefits on the $500 you paid.

MR. WALLIS: I think that's a very good point. The significance of that is that if the government is going into a welfare program, it will make a tremendous amount of difference just how it goes into it.

Consider education. Suppose that in my example, where we had the private school and people paying $500 tuition, the government imposed a $500 tax and then handed each citizen a voucher good for $500 toward tuition in any school where he might send his child. That would make all the difference in the world. Then, when a citizen got the notion he wanted his child to go to a $600 school, he would turn in the voucher and add the $100 from his own pocket.

There are many, many cases where government welfare programs are handled in that way, where private additions can be made. I am not sure to what extent that will be possible under the medicare system. Apparently under the national health system in England it isn't really practical.

HERBERT STEIN, Brookings Institution: I don't know to what extent you are regretting the fact that the government is not an innovator of new products in the sense in which you defined products. It seems this might be considered a useful division of labor, for the government not to be inventing education or medical care. But the government does have a product, which is income redistribution, and it invents or innovates methods of doing this. It makes decisions about the extent to which it is doing this. Your discussion was very muted on the subject of the income distribution aspects of a welfare problem. We do seem now to have under consideration welfare systems which are more purely income redistributional, without involvement in the question of innovation of products or the determination of ways in which people spend their money.

I wonder whether you would comment on the contribution that government may make with this kind of product, income redistribution.

MR. WALLIS: Maybe I should say explicitly I didn't mean to imply that there isn't any service the government can render that couldn't be handled through the market some way. There certainly are a number. I emphasized that all I am claiming was that a considerable number of important programs can be interpreted and understood in this fashion. Insofar as the programs fit into this analysis of political entrepreneurship you can anticipate in advance that there is going to be a big reduction in the total amount of resources available. While I said earlier I predicted as much to medical administrators at our place, I think a more accurate statement would be that I suggested it tentatively. I can't say that I really had such firm belief in this theory that I think you can predict it like the laws of physics.

But this prediction for expenditures on health seems to have come true, as I indicated, to a degree that I consider incredible. I would certainly limit my claim for this theory. I would not claim that it can explain everything the government does. As I indicated earlier, I think that if this theory is investigated I think one of the important things is to try to find out in what areas this type of machinery is likely to be governing. There is also the point already brought up that there are ways of doing the same thing which may get around the retardation effect.

WALTER WILLIAMS, Office of Employment Opportunity: I would like to pursue a point on the question before last. Your argument in education, as I understand it, is that when you substitute essentially a good in kind it is difficult to make a marginal increment to that bundle. Two things are bothering me. This may be true in the short run, but if the market system is working fairly well and if the people want marginal increments, they will develop mechanisms to bring these marginal increments. For example, if I have a child who needs tutoring or I want my child to have French in school, where the public schools do not offer it, that subsidiary schools will be set up to facilitate this marginal mechanism.

The second point concerns your medical or medicare example. This is not a substitution in kind. This is a substitution of government insurance for private insurance. It does not follow, at least in theory, that a substitution of one form of insurance for another, where that insurance does allow marginal expenditures, would in fact bring about the kind of results you are saying.

So I would ask: Is there not another possibility, perhaps in line with your own argument, that the political entrepreneur happens to get into industries that are mature? Is that not another possible explanation, that you are merely seeing a very smart politician happening to hit a fully mature industry? As I say, I have great, great difficulty seeing that insurance substitution.

MR. WALLIS: I don't think politicians usually hit mature industries. I think there may be a tendency for politicians to come in when about 50 percent of the people are involved, because then you can get a majority vote once you get over 50 percent. You can often get popular support long before there is 50 percent participation, if it means enough to a third bloc; that is, 20 percent is a bloc big enough for almost any political entrepreneur to go after and 20 percent of the market in private industry is also big enough for anybody to go after seriously.

So I doubt that the politician is likely to wait until a program is fully mature, not unless all of these political entrepreneurs are pretty sleepy. They are trying to outdo one another and get in their bid before the other fellow gets his in. If they don't come out and propose this for the voters, then there is danger that the other fellow will. So they don't wait until a private program is mature, but they try to avoid going off prematurely before there are enough interested.

MR. WILLIAMS: I think you argued that essentially most children were in schools before it became a public good.

MR. WALLIS: Of course, literacy is not an adequate measure of education. People were spending money on education to the extent that virtually everybody was literate. It was over 90 percent both in England and in New York by the time education became free. Prior to that, the schools had been subsidized, beginning in 1812 in New York and in 1833 in England.

On your insurance point, to the extent that the government really takes over the insurance bills, that seems to me to be a clear-cut case of the mechanism I described.

People are paying the bill for insurance and now the government says it will pay it.

MR. WILLIAMS: But you have the incremental use. I think it is important, that the insurance program allows an incremental decision where one can add at the margin very, very easily, whereas in education, at least in the short run, it gets very, very difficult.

MR. WALLIS: Probably if this went on long enough there would be people offering totally different kinds of insurance policies, the sort that would pay for the private room or whatever the public policy won't pay for, perhaps to pay for the drugs. There isn't much public policies won't pay for, actually, so that there isn't much margin left for this incremental change.

At that point the resources that can be obtained from the federal government to support this insurance program will be constrained because, meritorious as it may be, there will be people competing for those funds for air pollution control, highway programs, and a million and one other programs. Certainly the critical point is whether or not there is room left for incremental expenditures by consumers that are genuinely incremental.

PATRICK BOARMAN, Director of Research, House Republican Conference: It seems to me you are saying that in a political system such as we have, under a market system, we have a decentralization of decision making which is compatible with our particular political system, that political entrepreneurship tends in the long run to erode the decision making that goes on in the market. Not only that, but there is an economic cost, namely, that we tend to get an absolute reduction in the kind of services that would have been provided if we had had more of the decision making in the market place.

This seems to place us in a dilemma in which our political system, its democracy, its representative government, and its political entrepreneurship, propels us toward more and more public decision making in the provision of these services and toward a further erosion of the market. But we have this political system. Is there any solution to this dilemma? Are we headed for more public decision making?

MR. WALLIS: You are jumping to the conclusion that Herb Stein touched on too, that there is an implication this is all bad. I suppose it certainly isn't all good; but as to how the public would evaluate the process if they understood it, I think that is hard to say. If these things happen slowly enough, the public gets used to them. The public just thinks that's the way life is and that's the way the world is. Take the British reaction to the National Health Service. Most of the criticisms are that it's wasteful, extravagant, and that too much money is being spent on drugs or eyeglasses. The government vigorously attempts to keep expenditures down on one thing or another at one time or another, but there is no notion of comparing the system against what might have been. The British don't even compare it with what is going on in other countries, which suggests that their expenditures are too low, not too high—though what they spend may be wasted.

It is my impression that the population of England is very well satisfied with the National Health Service and that if we get one like that here people will get satisfied with it too, bad as it may be compared to what could have been. I certainly don't see anything to suggest how politically to stop this kind of a movement. I don't predict that people will be terribly unhappy because, in general, I don't think that there is much evidence that people will be less happy in regimented societies, unless they are regimented so abruptly that they can see the difference. [Laughter.]

If it comes about gradually, it is natural and the people are reconciled to it. Their attacks on it are always aimed at small details. Once they don't like it, they say "It's those damned bureaucrats in Washington." They think that if they change from one batch of bureaucrats to another this may improve things, but usually the remedy of the new batch is more of the same.

In other words, if some particular program is obviously not working, nobody thinks we ought to scrap it. They think we ought to push it harder.

DR. BOARMAN: We could drift into a more-and-more-regimented society then, on this basis.

MR. WALLIS: There will always be a few old fogies that don't like it and remember the old days and so on. But by and large people get adjusted. However things are natural and they won't complain about it. If, as I say, they do complain, their complaints won't be aimed at what is fundamentally wrong.

JOHAN BENSON, House Committee on Government Operations: Last week Dr. Tobin made some comments about the negative income tax. I don't know whether you have had the opportunity to read his paper.

MR. WALLIS: No, I haven't. I have a copy, but it was only given to me after I came into the room tonight.

MR. BENSON: Anyway, I would be interested in your observations on this proposal.

MR. WALLIS: Well, I have heard of the negative income tax. [Laughter.] Since there is supposed to be another meeting next week when we are both here, and if that is what he talked about, why, between now and then I suppose I will have some things to say about that.

It certainly has, at least on the face of it, a considerable amount of appeal. There are also some obvious and very strong objections to it. But I think the people who emphasize them so strongly overlook the objections to the present system. The real issue is: Would it be better or worse than what we are doing now? Is it perfect and ideal?

One might look up the history of the poor laws in England and what happened on them. Why were people so unhappy with them? Exactly how did they work as far as that goes? And what changes were made in the plan and why?

MR. BENSON: Your observations bring out other points that might be spoken of. In all of these circumstances you do not get isolated cases where this is pure entrepreneurship. For the most part you will probably find a mixture of many factors, of which entrepreneurship may be only one. But those who wish to oppose the program will naturally mention that.

MR. WALLIS: This is true in business entrepreneurship too; that is, if you look at the success of the Xerox Corporation, it wasn't all because of the brilliant invention. The new product might explain why the industry did so well and why, if this company had gone broke, some other would have picked up the product and done well. But there is a lot more to the success of any particular enterprise than just the merit of its product. I would agree that there are usually several forces operating.

When you are selling a political product to the public and discussing it, you never can come right out and say "This is for your self-interest. This is a chance for you to get some money away from other people." You always say things like, "This is to avoid the indignity of having to show that you need it," or something of that sort. Everybody wants to avoid that indignity, particularly those who couldn't possibly show that they needed the help.

As long as that kind of argument has to be made, there is a limit on the kinds of programs that are likely to be devised. That is, the programs are going to have to have at least plausible rationalizations that suggest they would help the poor. It may take too much ingenuity to make up that kind of argument for some programs. I think that basically people want to bring welfare to those who are impoverished; that does play a role in some so-called poverty programs.

GERALD POLLACK, Department of Commerce: In listening to your discussion, I hear a general tone of criticism about these programs. You said in response to Herb Stein's question that these are not altogether hostile to income redistribution. I wonder if you could spell out in a more positive way what you think our society should do collectively for the large number of people who are still below what one reasonably might call the poverty level. By implication do you really mean to be against public education or governmental health insurance, for example?

MR. WALLIS: After having studied up some on the history of education for this talk, I am probably less enthusiastic about public education than I was a few weeks ago. What I would have said then, quite clearly, would have been that I would favor public education but it makes all the difference in the world how it is done; that is, that the government should not nationalize the industry; that the way to do it would be through some kind of a voucher system such as I alluded to here.

But there does seem to be some ground for questioning whether the people even need that, whether that really has contributed anything. Certainly, however, there will always be the kinds of cases you mentioned. I mentioned those children in Mississippi, for example. It is perfectly obvious that they are not going to go into the market and buy themselves enough care, or their parents aren't. I think on the whole the truth is that we don't know how to deal with that kind of problem.

We hear a lot of talk about the desperate plight of the poor, that we are going to have revolution if we don't do this or that or the other. That talk is on a par with a harangue that we are going to have thousands of people dying this year of leukemia if we don't appropriate a billion dollars by June. Well, that is true and we are going to have people dying of leukemia even if we appropriate $10 billion tomorrow to save them.

On problems of poverty I think there might be a chance of making progress if more real research were done in social science—just as I have faith that someday we will know how to do something about leukemia. There is a lot of plausible conjecture, a big program is launched, but no evaluation is ever made of these big public programs that is worth anything. Certainly no controlled experiments have been conducted where you take a group of children in Mississippi and an equivalent group in Arkansas and you help one and you don't help the other; or you help one in one way and the other another way. This isn't likely to be done. I think we could learn something about it if we could take these children and put them into institutions and feed them. We know that would help. Probably the only really large-scale, successful, conscious attack on poverty, which has been by far and away the most effective, has been the one conducted through the rise in the economy since the industrial revolution. Almost everybody used to live in the kinds of conditions that we now consider dire poverty.

Otherwise one of the most dramatically successful attacks was the one that John D. Rockefeller's General Education Board and later, Foundation launched on the south along about the turn of the century. John D. Rockefeller, from way back before the Civil War, had always been interested in the condition of the Negroes. When he got rich and decided that he shouldn't deal with symptoms any more, that he had enough resources to eliminate the causes, he set out in the south to help the Negroes. Pretty soon he decided one can't really help them unless one helps the whites too. Then, in looking into that, he decided it is no use working on a lot of these institutional things if something basic isn't done about health. So the Rockefeller group got concentrated on hookworm and yellow fever and malaria; it has been a long-range, sustained program, which has had dramatic results.

I would still come back to the point that basically we don't have the knowledge we need. To some extent, improvement would probably require institutional changes of a sort we are not prepared to make, like taking the children away from the parents in certain types of families and putting them into a better family or a better institutional environment, if we knew how to do that. I think on the whole not many of us are likely to support that.

HARVEY SEGAL, *Washington Post:* Dr. Wallis, do you regard increases in per capita expenditures as a proxy for progress and medical service?

MR. WALLIS: Well, obviously not, but it is probably a good indicator over short periods. I take it what you are getting at is that, as we go on, we may have the funds used inefficiently.

One of the things I didn't touch on was that the medicare and medicaid programs have added so much inefficiency to the medical system that it has probably more than consumed the 80¢ rise in real medical services per capita. This is one detail that came to my attention at our hospital the other day. It is now necessary to have a good deal of additional working capital to run the hospital because the government is such a slow payer. Also the hospital has added literally dozens of people to process forms and paperwork.

Now, the hospital doesn't care much. It builds the costs to the medicare program. But these expenses get counted into the dollar figures on health expenditures. I suspect, if you looked into it, you would find that what little real increase occurred last year was used up in this kind of thing. Certainly over a longer period that would become an important factor in keeping expenditures from measuring health services.

In education, the costs in public institutions seem to be much higher than in private ones, allowing for quality of education. Of course, that is awfully hard to evaluate too because, if you take a thing like the Chicago branch of the University of Illinois, which is reputed to have the highest cost per student in the country, that is largely because of the colossal capital investment they made and purposes other than educational were sought in the capital investments, so it is not really fair to attribute all of that cost to education.

The interest rate used in calculating cost should be what capital can earn in our economy, not the rate on state bonds.

MR. TURE: With regard to what you said about total expenditures on medical care which resulted from the introduction of medicaid and medicare, what one fairly infers from this is that the popular attribution of the increase in the medical care component of the consumer price index to the introduction of medicare and medicaid is completely erroneous. The total outlay is on medical services.

MR. WALLIS: No. The increase in current dollars was almost fully accounted for by the increase in population and the increase in prices, so the per capital outlay in constant dollars increased scarcely at all. I think the figure went from $198.20 to $198.99, or something like that, from one year to the next. That is striking, for they had been rising steadily and then all of a sudden leveled off. I don't understand why the expenditures for medical care shouldn't have had at least, say, half the previous rise. That's why I think the figures can't be right.

Basically, the whole thing was a transfer from private to public; that is, public spending rose and private fell equally. Public spending did rise $4 billion, as I say, and the private spending fell about $3.3 billion in actual dollars. But that is the first time private spending had fallen in actual dollars for a long time.

MR. TURE: But then this surely could not have been the source of a very rapid rise in the major costs of medical care.

MR. WALLIS: Well, I certainly doubt that that part of the consumer price index is very accurate. That's an extremely difficult thing to measure, even if you had the National Bureau of Economic Research make a major project out of it and they haven't done that.

Basically there weren't any unmet needs, let me say, for medical care for the aged. When you look into studies of the aged like the one by Ethel Shanas of the National Opinion Research Center, and a couple of the others that were done at the same time, you find that they are very healthy nowadays compared to what they used to be. They are not healthy compared to people in middle life. They almost all have some kind of aches and pains which they take as natural for their age. Then, of those who are in need of medical care, most of them are getting it. This is partly because their income in retirement is far better than it used to be. There are private pension plans that have been going on for a long time and social security. Anyway, a lot of them past 65 are doing some work, earning some money, and so on. Their income is better than is usually thought, particularly because the dollar figures on income for the aged usually are not good; they are not comparable as measured in consuming ability to the same figures for middle-aged people.

Among those needing medical care but not getting it, a great majority don't trust doctors. They think if you go to the doctor he will tell you you've got cancer and then you'll die. So they stay away from him. And there is a prejudice against hospitals. This came out strongly.

Shanas calculated that 5 percent of those over 65 were not getting needed medical care for financial reasons. There are other data in the same book, however, which it seems to me would justify saying 8 percent. Five to 8 percent, let's say.

The basic point is that this program was instituted to meet a presumed enormous need that was not being met. But there wasn't any such unmet need. So all that happened was that the bill got transferred from those who had previously been paying it. I would predict, however, that the consumption of services will go up, now that the services are relatively free. This is another reason I find it hard to believe that total spending slowed down as abruptly as the preliminary government figures show.

MR. TURE: How important, how central to your findings, is the observation that as a result of the substitution of the public physicians' services for private activity the total volume of expenditures is likely to fall? (Inaudible remark.) That troubles me very much.

The first consequence of a substitution of public activity for private activity usually has been thought to be a change in the distribution and the consumption of the commodity or services. The second likely result usually expected is an increase rather than a decline in total consumption because the price constraint is no longer operative with respect to the demands for the service. On the supply side, the supply constraints don't have anything to do with cost of production, unless you assume that the government really has a whole shadow pricing system.

MR. WALLIS: Yes, I think that is the common belief. I think the common belief both in this country and in England about the National Health Service is that the thing is just hopelessly out of control and is bankrupting the British empire and all because the British have gone hog wild on medical care. But when you actually look at the figures, the total expenditures on health care in England have grown less since that was put into effect than they were growing before. And they have grown far less than in other countries. This does suggest that in fact health care in England has been retarded. I think a similar thing is noticeable in education.

Reflecting on these two empirical phenomena led me to wonder if there isn't a general principle working there. I think there is. Congressmen will tell you, as if it shows how stupid and irrational their constituents are, that the same constituents who write them one day saying "Don't raise taxes" write them two days later saying "For goodness' sake, put that new culvert in my neighborhood." Naturally the congressmen think this is inconsistent. Well, it doesn't seem to me that it is at all.

If my share of the cost of the culvert is $100, I might well be willing to pay $100 in taxes for that. But if the $100 in taxes is going to go to control air and water pollution in Alaska, I may protest to my congressman. You might think I am kidding, but I was in Alaska and ran into an air pollution team from the federal government up there. When I asked them if there was any air pollution they said "No, of course not, and we don't want to have any—" [laughter] "—that's why we're here." [Laughter.] So, feeling that some of my money will go to control air pollution in Alaska, I am not so enthusiastic about the tax increase as I am about the culvert.

I am very conscious that people do feel the way you do because, as you know, I am involved with administrators of higher education these days. Almost to a man they are certain that if they can tap the public treasury, all their financial problems will be solved. And they pretty much don't care how they tap it.

Now, as the head of a private institution, naturally I am eager to tap the public treasury, but I think it makes all the difference in the world, from a long-run point of view, how it is tapped. What most of administrators want is direct grants to institutions. They want the state or federal government to single out their university as a great institution to receive $8 million a year, or even $800,000.

State aid to private education has been extremely effective in New York and has left the schools completely independent. Probably a lot of you are from New York state and you know what their system is. The state gives direct grants to something over 300,000 students. Anybody in the top 10 percent of high school students on a statewide exam can get up to $1,000 toward tuition. There is a needs test. Anybody who can get admitted to a college can get up to $500, again subject to a needs test. And now they are proposing to give a bounty to every college for the number of degrees awarded, proposing $400 for each bachelor's or master's degree awarded, and $2,400 for each doctor's degree.

Now, aside from the deteriorating effects this will have on the standards for degrees—[Laughter.]—which will certainly be there, it seems to me a far superior system to direct grants.

Most of the administrators don't like it nearly as well, because the grant seems so easy. The government has all that dough. And if it hasn't got it, it can easily get it. That's obvious. Even the state of New York can easily raise a billion dollars by just snapping its fingers. And the federal government doesn't even have to snap its fingers or raise an eyebrow. So the administrators just think of its raising its eyebrow for their particular billion dollars. They don't think about all the other people who will be wanting an eyebrow raised, or about the fact that they just won't get a billion for this particular purpose, or about the possibility that the total amount may be cut down and private spending may be reduced by the availability of the public money.

MR. LEVINE: Two questions or comments on the medicare problem you brought up. You said you didn't believe your medical statistics. I wasn't going to question them any further, but since you want to explain them even though you don't believe them—[Laughter.]

MR. WALLIS: They are federal figures, so they must be right. [Laughter.] Incidentally, though, they have one interesting little characteristic. They have a component for private and a component for public, and each one is given as five significant digits. [Laughter.] So if it might be $30 billion, $792 thousand—

MR. LEVINE: There is the diseconomy of rounding.

MR. WALLIS: But then it is rounded to thousands. And when you add the two together, they come out to just precisely $40 billion on the nose. [Laughter.]

MR. LEVINE: I'm not questioning that it could.

MR. WALLIS: It could happen. [Laughter.] It's hard to understand. It suggests somebody started with a total and then he allocated it.

But why in the world would he start with that total, which is no bigger than the year before? I know lots of government figures are made up that way, by just sort of estimating. In this case the statistician would perhaps have extrapolated the rate of rise in the past.

MR. LEVINE: We may be carrying out an exegesis on a typographical error. [Laughter.]

MR. WALLIS: No, I don't think it's that. [Laughter.]

MR. LEVINE: Nonetheless, whatever the change was,

I have a strong impression that medical costs in the short run are pretty much controlled on the supply side in real terms, in constant dollar terms.

MR. WALLIS: What gives you that impression?

MR. LEVINE: The impression that medical services and facilities are fairly well saturated. If the medical care didn't change in real terms it might be well worth looking at the supply side for an explanation.

MR. WALLIS: On the idea that they are running at capacity?

MR. LEVINE: Whatever passes as capacity in this field, yes.

MR. WALLIS: Well, that would certainly be a possibility. You would expect that if that were the case, a tremendous price rise would occur in that period. I don't know whether prices increased much faster than normally. I am pretty confident that this is not the case, and particularly confident that it is not true that there was no increase in capacity from that year to the next.

This has been a period of extensive hospital building, of expanding the output of medical schools. A large number of new medical schools have opened up in the last decade.

MR. LEVINE: You're talking about a one-year change here.

MR. WALLIS: Well, these medical schools are in business and they are turning out their graduates. And the hospitals are being built and opening up and going into business. There are some shortages, of course, of personnel. Where they are underpaid, there are shortages. Nurses are a good example.

This supply side is certainly a possibility worth examining more closely. But without examining it, from the things I know or the impressions I have, I would be very surprised if the supply side provided the explanation.

MR. LEVINE: You may be right. This is just a guess of mine on the supply system.

MR. WALLIS: Well, it's an interesting guess.

MR. LEVINE: I have the impression that the major rationale for medicare was redistribution for those whose medical costs relative to their incomes are relatively high, whether because their incomes are low or their medical costs are high. If this is the rationale, then the fact that few people in the base here were not cared for does not explain away the reason for the program.

MR. WALLIS: The Shanas study showed that those who really were sick, the ones who really had substantial bills, were mostly getting free service already. My impression from the time when medicare was being argued politically was that it fits right into this theory about political entrepreneurship. It was felt that increasingly the burden of this cost was going to fall on the children, the middle-aged children of people who had elderly parents. This study throws some light on that; that isn't true either.

But this is very relevant: The children, that is, middle-aged people, when asked if they could cope with their parents' medical bills, gave much smaller estimates than the parents did of what the parents could cope with financially. They generally gave a rather high estimate of the probability of their having to meet the bills. The elderly people were asked, "Could you turn to your children?" And then when they were asked, "Are you likely to or would you under such circumstances?" they generally said "No." There was a big discrepancy there.

From the point of view of the political entrepreneur, all he needs to know is that these middle-aged people think that they are living under the shadow of the threat of some big medical bill. If they are and the political entrepreneur says I'll pick up those bills for you and protect you from that, then entrepreneurship works from his point of view.

Discussion of medicare went on so long, of course, that it's hard to remember all the arguments. Probably some of them were reversed by the end. It went on for 15 years or more. I don't remember all of them. But I do remember this particular one as playing a fairly definite role in the discussion, the probability of middle-aged people having to pay for their parents. The middle-aged people considered that risk substantial, at any rate, substantially greater than the elderly people considered it.

CARL COAN, Housing Subcommittee of the Senate: I've been wondering here how far you would stretch your topic to cover other subjects, and I'm thinking in terms of my own Subcommittee on Housing. The President is proposing to embark on a tremendous big subsidy program for housing, in which he says the federal government will help subsidize up to six million units over the next ten years.

Would you say that by the government becoming involved in subsidizing that many units that the net result would be that we will have less housing than we would have otherwise?

MR. WALLIS: That seems to me likely in the housing case, yes. Everybody will feel that he shoud get one of those subsidized houses. And there won't be anywhere near the number of houses they think there should be. There will be a lot more jockeying for those. This will probably result in boosting the price, in indirect ways, not the actual cash payment. This, again, is one of those factors presenting a good opportunity for building a real national political party for the first time. The allocation of those housing units would be very useful in terms of getting some party discipline on a national scale.

The record of the housing program to date is pretty dismal. That is, public housing programs have displaced a large number of low-income people and housed a small number of middle- and upper-income people.

THIRD SESSION

MR. WALLIS: With regard to the summary that Mr. Tobin gave of my paper, there are only two points with which I would really take exception. I realize, of course, he cast it in a different tone than I did but that is his right when he referred to the political entrepreneurs as demagogues. I think I avoided using that term and it is not at all clear to me that it is fair. That would require some analysis as to what you think is the proper role for a politician. Maybe he is rendering a useful service.

At any rate, I gave some thought to that kind of issue and decided that it doesn't seem to me really fair to politicians to identify political entreprenuership with demagoguery.

Professor Tobin also said that the reason politicians don't bring new services is because they aren't imaginative. My point was rather that, however imaginative they are, they can't get a chance to try out a new service unless they convince the customers in advance. If the politicians have the inspiration that an electric carving fork is what everybody needs, they have to persuade the customers before they can go into the business and bring it to them.

I am grateful to the reference to Shumpeter. My illusion was simply to the specific term and I will admit I came across Tullock's use of that only a few days before my paper was written. I don't pretend to any familiarity with the literature at all. In fact, in preparing the paper, I got the idea there is a good bit of literature that sounds pretty interesting.

Jim referred to the fact that finally we seem to be recognizing, as a consequence of the Negro civil rights movement, that Negroes count equally as people. I think some people are coming to recognize that. I don't think we've made a great big dent on the total problem. But where I would disagree with him would be in attributing the increased awareness to the Negro civil rights movement. It is just the other way around in my judgment. The Negro civil rights movement is a result of the recognition by some people that at least sometimes some Negroes count almost equally, as almost people. But people have been forced to recognize this not so much by moral considerations as by economic considerations. They have just had to face the fact that Negroes are able to perform certain useful economic tasks at a higher level than the ones they have been performing. Specifically, you can lower your costs, if you bring Negroes into your enterprise with intelligence and imagination. Beginning about the time of the second world war, a good 75 years after the emancipation, this began to happen on a substantial scale. We saw it happening in northern cities. It was seldom people who recognized that Negroes count equally as people who gave them these jobs. It was people who realized that their own competitive situation made it desperately necessary to get their costs down somehow. They saw these Negroes unemployed, looking for jobs at 50 to 75 cents an hour where they were paying other people a dollar an hour for a poor job. Sometimes they couldn't get people at a dollar an hour. Naturally it occurred to them, why not split the difference with the Negroes? Offer them a nickel more and save on what you are now paying.

Afterwards, when it was a big success, people naturally told you they did it for moral or humanitarian reasons. I know of a number of cases where that is positively not true.

My point is I think the Negroes finally, after 75 years and in the face of obstacles that could properly be called insuperable, did succeed on their own in getting into the economy in a small way. Once they got in, Negro hiring spread. After it had spread pretty far and enough people had had contact with Negroes, enough whites began to be receptive to Negro claims that education in a different school, if it was separate, wasn't equal. There were a good many other things about the way Negroes were treated and nobody ever gave it a thought.

I will take up one other particular point that I thought of including in my written rebuttal to the paper. It was brought to mind again by some of Tobin's comments on my paper.

I wonder when we talk about justice and equality whether we really ought to focus exclusively on the dispensing of rewards to individuals directly. Take, for example, his saying that we must spend far more on the education of the uneducable than on the those that are highly educable. I wonder whether that would really make for equality and justice.

Some of the most highly educable people come from the most privileged backgrounds and are provided very expensive, long-drawn-out, highly specialized training. They are then able to do things that confer on the poor benefits far beyond anything that can be done by just trying to educate the poor. Is it justice and is it conducive to equality, then, to say we won't do that? Should we say we won't let that good, that benefit come to the poor that way; that it's got to come the other way; that what we can't get by educating the uneducable we'll skip rather than take this privileged character who is privileged by heredity to be a genius and by family to be wealthy, who is in a family which stimulates his interests and so on? Rather than give him still further advantages by all of this education, we are going to skip him and pour our money into educating the uneducable. Of course, if they are literally completely uneducable, the authorities won't go quite that far maybe. I don't know what the criterion is for judging educability.

I just wonder if we would really be advancing justice

or equality with that kind of approach. In fact, I wonder what Jim means by equality. Under what conditions could one have the kind of justice he was talking about where a reward is based only on the merit of the individual, and only that part of the merit that is due to himself somehow and not due to environment or heredity? I wonder whether we maybe don't need to give up that whole approach. The farmer finds that pouring the most fertilizer onto the most fertile soil often does the most for the farm as a whole. May that not be possible here?

DR. TOBIN: I think that it is a misunderstanding of my remarks on economic equality, or inequality, to attribute them to any kind of philosophical position about what is justice and what is equality in the deepest sense of the word. I don't think, in fact, that the word justice was used in the original paper.

The reason the subject came up was much more pragmatic. I have detected that a part of the resistance to the idea of a negative income tax, is the feeling of many Americans that it's a fair race, that the poor are the guys who didn't work as hard and lost out and that's just their tough luck. It is the idea that this is justice that I was trying to cast doubt on, not that I knew what justice was in any basic sense. I think one of the ethics of American society that people adhere to is the idea of equality of opportunity. So I was only tracing out a few more of its implications and pointing out that there is this other sort of American idea, too, that once you have equality of opportunity then you can let the rewards fall to those who run the race the fastest. My point was that this was not at all inconsistent with the kind of redistributional measure I was proposing. Let's not read too much into these things or think that I was proposing as a basic ethical principle that nothing short of equality was just. We know that everything we do in this regard is some kind of pragmatic compromise between equality in the distribution of income and wealth, on the one hand, and inequalities to give incentives to people to do their best, on the other.

I don't think there would be any disagreement between Allen Wallis and me on the basic idea that some people may, for empirical reasons, believe that you need to shade this compromise more in the direction of inequality and incentives and other people believe that you can shade it in the other direction. So it is not so much a matter of basic principle as it is a kind of pragmatic compromise there. Since I went to some length to propose a program which embodies incentives and which does not invert status but maintains ranks in income distribution, I don't think that I am guilty of ignoring the functions of incentives and of the inequalities that result from that.

The other purpose of my remarks on inequality was also pragmatic. That was to suggest that the degree of inequality that we presently have might turn out to be self-defeating. It might be destructive of the attachments to the basic values of the society by people who find themselves so far below the majority of the population.

Mr. Wallis referred at one point to looking at things just in terms of sheer power and strength. If you are going to try to run a society that is based on consent, on a common acceptance of values and an orderly process of decision making, then there is a limit to the degree of difference in status that can exist. I would prefer, I guess, to look at the problem in these rather more pragmatic terms than get involved in the discussion of rights and justice to which Mr. Wallis referred.

Every time somebody talks about the way government programs misfire—are ostensibly designed to aid certain people, they actually end up aiding quite different people—they mention the minimum wage law, agricultural subsidies, restrictions of entry into various trades and professions, and so on. So, to clear that out of a debate about welfare programs, I will say I'm against the minimum wage law, I am against the present system of agricultural subsidies, I am against the licensing of taxis in New York city, etc. I don't think any of that is really germane to the topic of the day.

Talking about the functioning of markets, Mr. Wallis says that if you look carefully into malfunctioning markets, you almost always find that at the bottom of the malfunctioning is some kind of governmental regulation or interference and that if these were removed then the market would function okay. Does he think that the legislatures of the several states and the politicians of the

Congress sprung these interferences out of their own heads into the market without any demands for them from the participants in the markets themselves? That is inconsistent with the political theory Mr. Wallis was espousing in regard to welfare programs.

Take the specific instance of variable annuities. It is not because the state legislatures autonomously assumed a sort of bullheaded opposition to the proposals of various forward-minded insurance companies to let them issue variable annuities. It is because the other insurance companies, which have much more power over the state commissions and the state legislatures, don't want them to.

When I have talked about the malfunctioning of the housing market, I have specifically mentioned a number of misguided governmental interferences therein. But these also didn't come about just by chance. Many of them were in response to the people of the market themselves. In fact, I think Mr. Wallis is now himself engaging in this extension of the purview of economics into wider realms. He might therefore admit that the economic entrepreneur should regard politics as part of the realm in which he operates and seek to induce the government to protect his position against competition.

Now, let me refer to the specific remarks about the negative income tax. I have no objection whatsoever to being associated with Milton Friedman in advocating a negative income tax. On the history of the matter, I believe, the proposal is initially due to Lady Rhys Wil-

liams in England. But history aside, Friedman's idea of
the negative income tax is not the kind of proposal I was
making. He would not give a guarantee of benefits at a
poverty-line standard to people who had no other income. Rather, he would give people half the value of
their unused income-tax exemptions. That is certainly
not as high a guarantee as I was talking about.

In addition, Friedman suggests that his proposal would
make it possible by expenditure of a few billion dollars
to get rid of $30, $40, $50 billion of welfare expendi-
tures, get rid of all social security, get rid of all other
welfare-oriented programs of the government; whereas,
I don't try to fool anybody that way. [Laughter.]

As stated in an earlier paper, we know that those programs have different purposes from the relief of poverty.
Social security has commitments in response to prior
contributions. So that to think that you can substitute
the negative income tax plan, and particularly one on
the scale that he is talking about, for a social security
system seems to me just ridiculous. Clearly you are not
going to be able to solve the poverty problem by substituting a few billion dollars of expenditure for $40 or
$50 billion of expenditure.

What I would do is to substitute the negative income
tax for direct categorical public assistance payments as
they now exist. I would count the benefits under social
security and other transfer programs as part of the income base on which the entitlement of people to benefits
under the negative income tax plan is computed.

That is the reason that I was giving the figure of $20-$25 billion, a net figure after the cost of public assistance is subtracted, as the cost of my plan, and that is why it is much higher than the figures for plans that Allen Wallis was apparently referring to.

LOUIS DOMBROWSKI, *Chicago Tribune:* Dr. Tobin, isn't the negative income tax as you propose it merely substituting one form of social giveaway for another?

DR. TOBIN: I guess the short answer to that question is yes. [Laughter.] I don't know what the implication of the question really is. But in regard to social giveaways the question is whether the criteria of eligibility for them, make sense, whether they provide giveaways to people who need the giveaways, whether they provide giveaways in a way to preserve incentives, and so on. I tried to list in my paper two weeks ago some desirable principles of giveaway programs. I tried to point out how present giveaway programs violate those principles, how a kind of cash guaranteed income with incentive provisions—the sort of thing that is summed up in the negative income tax—meet those principles.

So the short answer to the question is yes and the longer answer to the question is: What's wrong with that? We are going to have to have giveaway programs and we ought to have them better, more efficiently organized, more appropriate to our basic objectives.

But I will comment on the word "giveaway" because of the self-righteousness involved in saying that. When someone is on the wrong side of zero with respect to the federal government, what you give to him is a giveaway; but when a guy is able to claim all kinds of tax deductions from the federal government, so he pays a lot less taxes than his neighbor, so long as he is not receiving public assistance, you don't consider that a giveaway. In a sense, somebody who doesn't pay as much taxes as you do or as I do is gaining at our expense; he is not paying the same share of the common expenditures of the government that we are. Yet somehow the society has arranged things so we don't regard that as in any way stigmatizing him. But, as soon as he gets to the point where the algebra of his transactions with the government turns from positive to negative, then we feel very self-righteous and talk about giveaways.

That is why we call the peanuts we give to the poor mothers on aid to dependent children giveaways, while the tax deductions given as oil depetion allowances are just the clear rights of businessmen.

CARL COAN, Housing Subcommittee of the Senate: Might I ask you, Mr. Wallis, whether you wouldn't consider the negative income tax as having a type of free enterprise element involved in it? Effectively you are providing a family with a given income, giving it wide latitude in expenditure without having the heavy hand of government watching over its shoulder to see how it is spent.

MR. WALLIS: I indicated that my presumptions are very favorable toward the negative income tax. The six criteria that Tobin gives that he thinks a good assistance program should meet all seem to me valid. It is better to give relief in cash than in kind but in his paper Dr. Tobin spelled out why it is and it was along the lines you have indicated. A thousand dollars given to a family in cash will certainly buy a good deal more welfare than a thousand or probably two thousand dollars ladled out by social workers. I don't think there is any question about that. I would like to ask Dr. Tobin this question:

What are the main objections to the negative income tax that need to be taken seriously? What are the answers to those objections? Maybe there are some which a man like Friedman, who is a great advocate of a similar program, admitted in the quotation I read that he didn't see any answer to. Everything has objections. You hardly ever have a program you can advocate and say there isn't one single consideration to be taken seriously that weighs against it. There always are some.

I feel that Tobin brought out very well the positive side of it. I also have the feeling that his points fitted in with my presumptions and therefore he didn't teach me a lot, but I haven't heard it seriously attacked. Most of the attacks I hear on it are just like he said: they aren't reasonable. They come either from people who don't want to achieve what it is aimed to achieve or from people who misunderstand it or from people who say because it isn't perfect we don't want anything to do with it, people who refuse to weigh it against the alternatives. On all of those scores it sounds very good to me, but I would like to hear the serious arguments against it analyzed.

DR. TOBIN: The political argument that you quoted from Friedman I don't regard as a serious argument against it. I have been hearing ever since I can remember that the whole political process is going to be subverted in the United States by the fact that the government, beginning with the New Deal, was engaged in welfare programs which were buying votes. It would be impossible ever to put such a government out of office, I was told. I haven't observed that this is in fact what has happened to the political process and I don't think it would happen under this program either.

It is already possible to imagine that you could put together a majority behind a candidate who promises to tax the minority for their benefit. I can imagine lots of majorities that might be assembled on that basis. Yet the political process doesn't seem to work that way because it isn't that kind of pure majority rule. The interests of the various people who might be in such a coalition are not that identical.

On economic grounds, so far as I can tell, the main argument against the negative income tax would be this:

Some people, not now on welfare, who are now subject to a zero marginal tax rate or to the first bracket tax rate of the regular income tax would be subject to a much higher marginal tax, namely, the marginal tax rate under the negative income tax, say 50 percent or

33⅓ percent. The incentive effects here may be unfavorable, though the incentive effects for the greater number of people now on welfare at the low end of the scale are favorable. It is not that anyone is going to be made worse off by the scheme but it is just that the marginal tax rates of some will be higher.

In several cities in New Jersey, the Wisconsin Poverty Institute is sampling families and subjecting them to this kind of treatment. When their study is completed maybe we will know more about this particular problem.

WALTER GARVER, U.S. Chamber of Commerce: While the negative income tax may provide more freedom in spending cash it would also give some more welfare than they are getting now. I believe Mr. Tobin said he thought the aim of this thing was to increase the probability for opportunity. What bothers me is that these things could be more restrictive rather than giving more freedom, because the majority rule will still decide, I think, what is welfare and make restrictive or coercive provisions. When it comes to education, I think we've got good precedent already in our history for saying that when you get a certain amount of education you owe the society something in return. One not only has given people probabilities for education but expects a return to society from it, and I think this could become coercive.

MR. WALLIS: I think it is certainly true that we expect people who have benefited from education to pay back a lot more. Being connected with a private institution which depends greatly on voluntary contributions, I know we certainly do get a lot of generous support of exactly that character. We are not able to use compulsion to get it, but these people either have some kind of internal compulsion or else we are just terribly persuasive in our approach to them.

The argument that compulsory education has led to more education than people had otherwise doesn't seem to hold up very well in investigations that have been made of that. There has been an effort to see what the effect of the school-leaving age is on the average amount of education, state by state. People have worked this out by a regression analysis. There are a lot of things that affect the age at leaving school, such as the prospects of earning money from education, the income to pay for it, educational background, and so on. But when you take all of these into account in a multiple regression you don't find anything left that is explained by the laws from state to state. The variation among states is no more fully explained when you do take account of what the law is about the school-leaving age than when you don't.

I think we should compel everybody to have some type of social insurance because, if he doesn't provide for himself, we will then feel obligated to look after him. We are not content to say, "Well, it's his own fault he is lying in the gutter starving, so let him die," and particularly not "let his children die." We are not content to do that, so the argument is made, therefore, that we are going to force everybody in the country to take this type of insurance.

Here we must get some idea of what the facts are. How many would really fail to make adequate provisions for whatever it is that is involved? This argument about compelling insurance sounds pretty good. It is used around universities with regard to compelling people to contribute to retirement plans. If some professor retires and is starving, the university isn't willing to put up with that; so they just put up some money for him. They say they have to protect themselves against that. Now, the number of starvation cases I would guess would be extremely small, probably no greater than the number we have anyhow.

The quantitative issue seems to me extremely important before you legislate 100 percent compulsion. Would the public begin to move in and legislate how families collecting on the negative income tax should spend it? I suppose there is a possibility of that, but I think it would be a whole lot less than under the present set-up. That is, they might move in and say "anybody who buys any beer can't collect any more negative income tax," or whatever it is the public is against at the moment. But that doesn't strike me as a high probability, nothing like what we see as a fact under the existing welfare programs.

CARL MADDEN, U.S. Chamber of Commerce: If the proposal of Professor Tobin would reduce the rate of growth, would he still favor it? Or, to put the question differently, he seems to think that his program would increase welfare. What does he mean by welfare and would the program increase it? How does he deal with Mr. Wallis' argument that a more rapid rate of growth is the most effective weapon against poverty?

DR. TOBIN: I don't think I have to deal with that argument since I agree with it. A more rapid rate of growth is the most effective weapon against poverty. I have said so many times and I will say it again. I guess, to use an answer that I have heard on such occasions before, I would have to say that I don't agree with the question. [Laughter.] I don't see any significant conflict between a welfare program of this kind and a satisfactory rate of growth. I don't think that we are faced with the kind of choice that you are trying to present to me.

MR. MADDEN: I thought I heard Mr. Wallis say that increasing the education of the educable might be more productive than increasing the education of the uneducable. I thought there was a difference of opinion between you two on the question whether the program you advocate would, in fact, increase productivity.

DR. TOBIN: I don't understand, because nothing I proposed was designed to stop the gifted man with inherited wealth or well-to-do parents from going to a law school or getting a Ph.D. in physics.

If you look at the Coleman Report on Education, you can see that there are immense differences by socio-economic status, by race, by residential location, the region of the country, and so on, in the percentage of children at every grade who score up to certain levels on standard tests of reading skill or arithmetic skill.

I regard those differences in probability among groups so defined as evidence of inequality of educational opportunity. I would be led to think we had done a good job on equality of educational opportunity if another Coleman Report some years from now, in which the same kind of ex post probabilities were computed, were to show that those probabilities did not depend on these environmental factors.

That doesn't mean it is possible or that one can or should spend a lot of resources to bring every individual, regardless of his initial genetic IQ, whatever that means, to the same level as every other individual. It only means that belonging to a particular demographic group or coming out of a particular socio-economic stratum shouldn't change the probabilities in the large of individuals scoring well on tests. We ought to allocate educational resources, if we really mean to take equality of opportunity seriously, in the direction of trying to diminish and eventually to eliminate those differences. I don't see how that is going to interfere with the development of the skills and productivities of the gifted students of any socio-economic class.

PATRICK BOARMAN, Director of Research, House Republican Conference: Professor Tobin, I can understand and accept the economic efficiencies of the negative income tax as a method superior to the existing methods of dispensing welfare, but don't we have a problem here in that we institutionalize poverty, that we build it into the tax system? We make it somehow respectable, or at least more respectable than it now is. The merit of existing methods of giving welfare is that there is something slightly disreputable about it. If you are on welfare, this is not good. But if you are the beneficiary of a negative income tax, why, this is fine. This is just the other side of the coin. Do we not get rid of the scrutiny, testing whether people are really making an effort to get out of poverty?

In other words, the negative income tax, it seems to me in that psychological sense, reduces the incentive to get out of poverty. The level of the minimum payment that we make under the negative income tax may be expected to rise. How far no one can say. It depends on the political process. But, could we not end up with a society which consists of a large number of people who are not really working, are not earning, and another group of people who are earning and supporting those on the negative income tax with all of the consequent jealousy and envy and injustice that results? Would this not perhaps represent a deterioration from the situation that now exists in the welfare field? Aren't we risking here the very destruction of the consensus that you seem to be trying to get on the part of those who are in the so-called poverty class?

DR. TOBIN: If it all worked as badly as you say, then I suppose it would have the consequences you fear. The only saving grace then, as against the present system, would be that at least the people involved would have more to eat. Their needs would be better provided for than they are now.

I think that empirically it doesn't seem to be true that the stigma of being on welfare, or the surveillance and scrutiny that you refer to, have been effective incentives for people to get off the welfare rolls. The fact that it hasn't worked that way enables Mr. Wallis to refer to a "welfare explosion." Perhaps the reason it doesn't necessarily work the way you said is that there is a certain demoralization and dependence that is built up by this scrutiny, by this stigma, by the surveillance in the present system. So people just don't muster the capacity and motivation to escape it. My guess as to the way people behave is different from yours; I wouldn't expect the system to have the results you talked about. Rather I would expect that the number of people on the negative side of the tax system would gradually diminish with general economic progress and with the workings of the incentives themselves.

KIRKLEY COULTER, Senate Antitrust and Monopoly Subcommittee: There seems to be a sort of unspoken assumption here that whatever expenditures may arise out of this or other programs will be automatically balanced by taxation. That is to say taxes will have to be levied to meet these expenditures.

Is there not a danger that, having decided we would like to give expanded welfare to the poor, you may then have trouble through the decision-making machinery of our government in also deciding to levy the taxes to raise the money to do it? You may face the problem of a deficit, perhaps a mounting deficit, that you somehow can't cope with. At the moment we seem to be in a sort of a dead center on the whole budgetary process. There are those who say we must raise taxes. There are those who say we must reduce the expenditures, and also perhaps those who say we should do both.

Almost everyone seems to agree that we should do something, one or the other or some combination, to reduce the size of the deficit that would otherwise result. But I am not at all sure that we really will. Is there not a problem that the decision-making apparatus of our government will be unable to face up to this and will in fact simply give us a ratio of revenue to expenditures which is not decided consciously but is merely the result of a sort of process of drift rather than decision?

DR. TOBIN: I think there is a real problem, as you say, and as the present circumstances may exemplify, in getting Congress to gear fiscal policy to the demands of the economic situation. I think that is a problem we are going to face all of the time anyway. I don't particularly see that proposals like this change the nature of that problem. I can hardly imagine that a negative income tax would be adopted in one fell swoop by the Congress without some rough matching with additional tax revenues. We are always going to have this problem of matching taxes and expenditures, or fitting the deficit or surplus of the government budget to the circumstances of the moment. I just can't see why this makes it any worse, unless you imagine that you could get votes in Congress to put in a program like this with the clear idea that it was all going to be deficit-financed. That I don't think is going to happen. It is going to be squeezed into the budget either from the growth in the revenues of existing taxes or from foregoing a tax cut that otherwise would be possible, say, at the end of the war.

JOHAN BENSON, House Committee on Government Operations: In thinking about the nightmare conjured here by Dr. Boarman, I wonder what would be your consideration if tied to this negative income tax there were a concept of the government being the employer of last resort, that is, these people would be pressed into some kind of work or training which could help them to rise out of their helpless situation?

MR. WALLIS: I don't have an answer to that really. This idea of the government becoming an employer of last resort does make some presumptions about the facts. You often hear it said that there are a lot of able-bodied people drawing welfare payments. The few attempts that I have been able to make to look into that in a very small or local way suggest there aren't really as many of them as you hear. When you get right down to it, they are rather scarce. So I don't know whether establishing the government as an employer for a relatively small number would be a worthwhile venture. Offhand I doubt very much that that would add appreciably to the value of the scheme. It may be the kind of thing that would come up. People who are drawing the negative income tax would be under more and more pressure, say, to get education or training. There would be lots of talk about what is wrong with them and what can be done about them. There doesn't appear to be much of anything that can be done about the people in that category. You might have some hope for their children but even that is not a good generalization. There is so much variation among these people as individuals.

DR. TOBIN: I think there are two different ideas associated here. One is some kind of requirement on recipients of welfare payments or negative income tax payments that they enlist in training programs or take jobs that are found for them. The other is that the government stand by as an employer of last resort for anybody who hasn't been able to find another job, such persons would show up at some place in the city and get paid a certain wage and assigned to do work.

You could combine the two ideas and say that the clients of the employer of last resort would include not only those who came there voluntarily but those who were pushed there by the requirements placed on recipients of public assistance. Let us keep the two prongs of the idea distinct. They could be combined or they could exist separately, one or the other or both.

The spirit of the negative income tax, I think, is the carrot idea rather than the stick. People will have incentive to take jobs and to participate in training programs without any such condition on the receipt of public assistance. The threat is a very difficult one to carry out, the threat that unless you do so and so we will take away all of your negative income tax or all your public assistance and your family can starve. Then there would be lots of problems of adjudication as to whether an individual really did refuse to go to work, or whether he really did refuse to go to manpower training, and if so whose fault it was, etc., etc.

I prefer to rely on the incentive provisions, and to make the training and job opportunities, etc., available to be used without the kind of penalty of reduction of welfare benefits.

As to the employer of last resort proposal, I find it hard to imagine just how that would operate. Could people who don't have any other job on a particular day just show up somewhere and get a job for which they will get paid? There will be great difficulty in organizing and providing real work, so that some tasks of significance are carried out. Nobody would know how many people, what kind of people, what kind of a work force you are going to have from day to day. It would be very hard administratively to differ from a disguised relief program. The program as a disguised relief program is not a very good substitute for the negative income tax. There isn't the same kind of test of need based on family income, family size and composition, and so on that you would have under the negative income tax.

Sometimes the employer of last resort idea is defended

by the observation that there are a lot of tasks that need to be done, even requiring only unskilled labor, in all of our cities. Keep the parks and streets cleaner.

But the way to get those tasks done and to hire people to do them is to appropriate more money for those purposes. That would be better than a mobile and unstable work force.

JAMES A. LANIGAN, House Committee on Government Operations: To what extent would the negative income tax shift to the federal government welfare burdens now carried on by private charity and state and local governments?

DR. TOBIN: It would shift to the federal government almost all of the public assistance programs now carried on by state and local governments. Most of those are now carried on with federal sharing, so that is not a complete shift. But there would be some relief to the budgets of states and localities.

Some states and localities might wish to give higher standards of benefits because their areas have higher than average costs of living. My proposal would be that they be allowed to do that, provided it is done within the general structure and rules of the negative income tax scheme, and that the federal government participate fractionally in that supplementation. Aside from that, it would be a federal program. Some expenditures now made by states and localities would be saved by the states and localities. As to what happened to private charity, that is up to private charity.

As far as the negative income tax proposal is concerned, I think that receipts of private charity should be counted as income for the purpose of the 50 percent tax or the 33 percent tax or whatever it is that determines the size of benefits received from the federal government.

MR. LANIGAN: Would the proposal then have the effect in some states of lowering the total amount of welfare money available for welfare?

DR. TOBIN: Yes. I think it is probable that the national standard that would be embodied in federal legislation, at least in the first instance, would be lower than the theoretical maximum budget of the highest aid-to-dependent-children states or localities. That is why I mentioned the possibility that some states might wish to supplement the national minimum standards by a higher standard, either because they have a higher cost of living or because they have a greater sense of responsibility. This should be done in a way which would preserve the eligibility rules and incentive provisions of the general scheme, and the federal government would share the cost of that supplementation.

MR. WALLIS: That question does bring to my mind the tendency of variations in welfare payments to allocate the unemployed where they are most needed, so to speak, or where they are the least nuisance. I think of this particularly in relation to Rochester. Last night I heard the city manager complaining or maybe he was boasting, I don't know which, to the head of the Chamber of

Commerce that the Chamber of Commerce there is the only one he knows of that, when it puts out literature to people who may be thinking of moving there does not say, "Don't come here unless you have a skill" and does not say, "Don't come here unless you have the resources to support yourself for X weeks." Relief is available within ten minutes of arriving in town and the relief standards are quite high. The city is as prosperous as, if not more prosperous than, any other in the country. It has a severe chronic overemployment situation. The number of job vacancies runs about three times the number of unemployed. It is extremely rare for unemployment to hit 2 percent and is under 1 percent a good part of the time.

There have been studies made of the Negroes who migrated up there and they have been absorbed into employment very rapidly. They don't usually come straight from the south to Rochester. Most get there by two or three stages. They may get to St. Louis and then to Buffalo. Eventually they pick up word about Rochester and they go there.

So I think probably these high relief standards and the generous terms do serve to recruit a labor force for the city. If relief were cut back as it undoubtedly would be under the negative income tax, I assume labor recruitment would be handled differently.

GEORGE IDEN, Joint Economic Committee staff: Men's motivations are affected by their relative income standing, which dictates whether they can afford a second-hand car and TV, while looking at someone else who cannot afford anything of the sort. It boils down to a matter of faith in humanity, more or less. Perhaps less work will be done in the economy or perhaps more, depending on how people's motivations are affected by shifting their relative income. Maybe society will say it is worth the cost to do so. I would appreciate it if Professor Tobin would care to comment on this expression of an issue as I see it.

DR. TOBIN: I think you stated it very well. That is indeed the issue. I would agree with your conclusion that whichever way it comes out we should be happy.

FOOTNOTES

FIRST LECTURE

[1] "Is a Negative Income Tax Practical?" (with Joseph A. Pechman and Peter Mieszkowski), *Yale Law Journal*, November, 1967.

SECOND LECTURE

[1] Ida C. Merriam, "Social Welfare Expenditures, 1929-67," *Social Security Bulletin*, December, 1967.

[2] A. V. Dicey, *The Relation Between Law and Public Opinion in England during the Nineteenth Century* (2d edition; London: Macmillan and Co., Limited, 1914). Introduction to the Second Edition, pp. lxiv-lxv.

[3] The Senate majority leader at that time, who played a major part in weakening the bills, is now President, and in his present office assumes much the same stance on these issues as have all of his predecessors of the past quarter-century.

[4] Suggested to me by George J. Stigler, who said that Aaron Director suggested it to him.

[5] Milton Friedman, "Social Welfare Measures," Chap. XI in his *Capitalism and Freedom* (Chicago: University of Chicago Press, 1962), p. 179.

[6] The ideas presented here came to my mind mainly as a result of reading E. G. West's *Education and the State* (London: Institute of Economic Affairs, 1965).

Gordon Tullock (*Entrepreneurial Politics* (Charlottesville: University of Virginia, Thomas Jefferson Center for Studies in Political Economy, 1962), p. 21, has used the terms "entrepreneurial politics" and "political entrepreneur":

> An individual may run for some office, offering a platform of some specific measures. Then he is a political entrepreneur. If, on the other hand, he unites with a number of other candidates, to present jointly a uniform program to the voters, then the "party" is the entrepreneur.

Tullock's emphasis is on the analogy between profit maximizing and vote maximizing, while mine in the present paper is on the innovative or new-product aspects of entrepreneurship.

[7] These facts and the quotation are from West, *op. cit.*

[8] The quotation and the other information about the development of public education in New York is from E. G. West, "The Political Economy of American Public School Legislation," *Journal of Law and Economics*, Vol. 10, 1967, pp. 101-28.

[9] Ethel Shanas, *The Health of Older People* (Cambridge: Harvard University Press, 1962), p. 92.

There would be a case for raising the ratio "one person in twenty," or 5 percent, in the first sentence quoted to one person in 12, or 8 percent. When people who reported that they had been ill but had not seen a doctor were asked why not, 5.6 percent said they could not afford a doctor; hence the figure in the quotation. At another point in the interview, however, "after detailed discussion of finances and the problems which older people faced in living on a limited income, all respondents were asked: 'Are there any things you especially need that you've had to do without because you don't have enough money?' . . . Only eight of every one hundred persons in the older population specifically said that they needed medical or dental care."

[10] Rita R. Campbell and W. Glenn Campbell, *Voluntary Health Insurance in the United States* (Washington: American Enterprise Institute, 1960), p. 1.

[11] Joseph Brenner, Robert Coles, Alan Mermann, Milton J. E. Senn, Cyril Walwyn, and Raymond Wheeler, "Children in Mississippi," in *Hungry Children,* a Special Report of the Southern Regional Council (5 Forsyth Street, N.W., Atlanta, Georgia), undated but apparently 1967, pp. 5-6.

[12] *The People Left Behind,* a report by the President's National Advisory Commission on Rural Poverty (Washington: Government Printing Office, 1967), p. 11.

[13] Rochester Bureau of Municipal Research (New York), *The Monroe County Penitentiary,* March, 1964. Rochester Bureau of Municipal Research (New York), *Justice Detained: A Pilot Study of Defendants Confined in the Monroe County Jail,* October, 1967.

[14] From the translation by William Mackworth Praed of Sophocles' *Chorus from Ajax.*

[15] Basic data from "Public and Private Expenditures for Health and Medical Care, Fiscal Years 1929-67," Research Note #21, Division of Health Insurance Studies, Social Security Administration, November 20, 1967.

Public expenditures in millions of 1967 dollars rose from $8,645 in 1965-66 to $12,640 in 1966-67, while private fell from $30,743 to $27,360, raising the total from $39,388 to $40,000. Per capita, the total was $198.16 in 1965-66 and $198.99 in 1966-67, while 1964-65 was $188.45. The 1966-67 data are preliminary estimates.

Although I had predicted—or, more accurately, suggested tentatively in conversations with a few medical administrators—that the medicare and medicaid programs would cause a slowdown in the growth of funds available for medical care, I nevertheless consider that the preliminary estimate for 1966-67 must be substantially below the correct value. It does not seem possible that expenditures that had been growing so fast for so long could have come to such a screeching halt as these data indicate.

[16] D. S. Lees, "Health Through Choice: An Economic Study of the British National Health Service," *Freedom or Free-for-all?* (Ralph Harris, ed.) (London: Institute of Economic Affairs, 1961), p. 76.

[17] A B.U.P.A. brochure dated January, 1968, for which I am indebted to Marion B. Folsom, who called my attention to B.U.P.A., asserts that "four major advantages are associated with private treatment in illness:

  "1. Arrangements can usually be made quickly and conveniently.

  "2. Freedom to have the specialist you and your doctor choose. . . .

  "3. A private room. . . .

  "4. Privacy and . . . greater freedom of visiting hours."

These are followed by a reference to "a warm and human service."

[18] West, "The Political Economy of American Public School Legislation," *op. cit.*

REBUTTALS

W. Allen Wallis

[1] William Graham Sumner, *What Social Classes Owe to Each Other* (Caldwell, Idaho: The Caxton Printers, Ltd., 1963), pp. 136-41. First published New York: Harper and Brothers, 1883, emphasis in original.

[2] George J. Stigler, *The Intellectual and the Market Place* (New York: The Free Press of Glencoe, 1963), p. 93.

[3] Bankers Trust Company, New York, *1965 Study of Industrial Retirement Plans.*

[4] "The Administration of Large Pension Plans," *Monthly Labor Review,* October, 1967, p. 49.

[5] Professor Friedman tells me that he no longer holds the view quoted here. His present view on the political hazards of the negative income tax is analogous to his basic position on the negative income tax, which is that while it is not good in and of itself, it is preferable to alternative ways of meeting the problem. Politically, he now argues, the negative income tax has its dangers, but they are less than the dangers associated with alternative programs.

DISCUSSION

FIRST SESSION

[1] Christopher Green, *Negative Taxes and the Poverty Problem* (Washington: The Brookings Institution, 1967).